5 Minutes *with* Christ

5 Minutes *with* Christ

Spiritual Nourishment for Busy Teachers

edited by

Lou DelFra, C.S.C., *and* Ann Primus Berends

of the Alliance for Catholic Education

University of Notre Dame

ave maria press AmP notre dame, indiana

Founded in 1865, Ave Maria Press is a ministry of the United States Province of Holy Cross.

www.avemariapress.com

ISBN-10 1-59471-275-1 ISBN-13 978-1-59471-275-3

Cover image © British Library/HIP/Art Resource, NY.

Cover and text design by Katherine Robinson Coleman.

Printed and bound in the United States of America.

Library of Congress Cataloging-in-Publication Data

5 minutes with Christ : spiritual nourishment for busy teachers / edited by Lou DelFra, Ann Primus Berends.

p. cm.

Includes bibliographical references and indexes.

ISBN-13: 978-1-59471-275-3 (pbk. : alk. paper)

ISBN-10: 1-59471-275-1 (pbk. : alk. paper)

1. Catholic teachers--Prayers and devotions. 2. Jesus Christ--Biography--Meditations. 3. Bible. N.T. Gospels--Meditations. I. DelFra, Lou. II. Berends, Ann Primus. III. Title: Five minutes with Christ.

BX2170.T43A13 2011

242'.68--dc23

2011026709

CONTENTS

INTRODUCTION

Living and Loving the Gospels

To know Jesus is to love Jesus. But how do we come to know Jesus?

To know Jesus more deeply is to love Jesus more deeply. But how do we come to deepen our knowledge of Jesus, and so to deepen our love?

Matthew describes the beginning of Jesus' public ministry like this: "[He] went throughout Galilee, teaching in their synagogues and proclaiming the good news of the kingdom" (Mt 4:23). Everything else that follows in the four gospels is, in a sense, a result of this activity, this daily life spent as a teacher. No wonder teachers have so readily and richly pondered the life of Jesus.

This is a book of reflections by educators, as educators in the Faith. From the interplay between the gospels on the one hand and the experiences of a community who spends its days in the classroom on the other hand, there vibrantly emerges here the person of Christ the Teacher, one of Jesus' most powerful and pervasive identities.

When I first began teaching, as a young layperson at a Catholic high school in Philadelphia, a priest at the high school suggested that I begin spiritual direction. Bristling with eagerness to become Christ's greatest disciple ever (I was, after all, a religion teacher!), I was up for anything to improve my spiritual life. I entered my first spiritual direction meeting and asked my director, "What spiritual masters should I read (I was, after all, an English teacher too!) to deepen my relationship with Christ?" His answer was swift and disarmingly simple: "I recommend four for starters: Matthew, Mark, Luke, and John. When you have them down, we can move on."

I suppose a lifetime of Mass attendance should have prepared me for such an answer. As a child, one of the many wonderful oddities of the Mass was that before the last reading, and only for the last reading, the organ suddenly blasted and everyone suddenly stood and sang, "Alleluia, Ah-ah-le-lu-ia, Ah-le-e-lu-u-ia!" The priest picked up a special golden-encased copy of the Scriptures, which had been mounted alone and prominent on the altar and not used by the other readers. Then came the booming, confident voice of our otherwise quiet and reserved pastor, "A proclamation of the Holy Gospel according to . . ." and then the whirlwind. I watched my elders quickly, almost secretively, sign the cross on their foreheads, lips, and hearts, some proclaiming "Glory to you, Lord" while others mumbled "May the words of the Gospel be in my mind, and on my lips, and in my heart." The most skilled congregants, like my grandmom, were able to say both the former out loud with the congregation and the latter, simultaneously, rapid-fire under their breath, not wanting to miss a syllable of their allotted prayer in this clearly singular moment. Here was high drama. Here was heightened attention. It was time to read the Gospel.

It was time to hear the stories of Jesus—the hyperbolic, apocalyptic, cut-you-to-the-bone images and sayings that filled me as a child with fear and wonder, but also intrigue, affection, and ultimately love. I listened intently to the Pharisee-defying confrontations and the crowd-stunning miracles that I dreamed about at night. I reflected on the mysterious birth, life, death, and resurrection of God-become-human, at once both stupendously awesome, turning the cosmos upside down, yet at the same time personal and totally intimate, concerning my life like nothing else.

Perhaps one of the surest signs of the gospels' mystery and inspiration is this: they are most definitely not one-time reads. We seem to know this instinctively. When was the last time you heard a gospel passage read and someone yawningly moan, "I've already heard that one"? The stories that captivated me in childhood still enchant, startle, and fortify me today. Since the day my spiritual director invited me to focus on the four evangelists, I have begun each day by reading the Gospel for that day's

Mass. I have been through the four gospels a number of times now, and I am somewhat surprised to realize that I am always eager to start over again the next year.

Sometimes my morning reading is an attentive approach, like a captivated student before a trusted teacher, open and wondering what healing or life-giving mystery Christ will reveal today. Sometimes it is a wary circling, for the object of attention often breathes words of fire, fierce justice, and fatal commitment. Sometimes I open the pages full of curiosity and desire; at other times dejected, hurt, and vulnerable; and still other times sluggish and distracted. *He* is always waiting there. Far from deadening, the result of this constant circling toward the person of Jesus through the eyes of Matthew, Mark, Luke, and John has been definitive and transformative. I have come to know Jesus more deeply through the stories of his life, death, and resurrection, and because of these stories I have come to love him more deeply.

This book is a collection of daily reflections—by teachers and for teachers—on the person of Christ the Teacher. Each meditation begins with a gospel passage and continues with an educator's reflection on that passage. The reflections are organized chronologically, tracing the journey of Christ from the announcement of his conception in the womb of Mary, through many of his teachings and healings, his journey to

Calvary, his death and resurrection, and to his final ascension back to the Father. The book is written in the belief that daily reflection on the person of Christ made manifest in the four gospels is one of the richest, most accessible, and most transformative sources of the revelation of God that we as a Church possess.

My life and vocation have led me to serve as the Director of Pastoral Life in a Catholic school teacher and principal formation program at the University of Notre Dame called the Alliance for Catholic Education (ACE). Maybe the only job that comes close to being as fulfilling, demanding, draining, inherently meaningful, exhilarating, and life changing as teaching is that of helping others to become great teachers too. In ACE, I have the great privilege of helping provide an educator-formation experience that will provide Catholic schools with not only highly effective classroom teachers and leaders, but also teachers—regardless of subject content—and leaders who will nurture the spiritual lives of their students and their schools.

ACE's formation program is centered on the gospels and the Eucharist—the life of Christ in word and sacrament. From the moment our teachers and principals enter the program, they are introduced to the person of Christ the Teacher. Our teachers begin their first day in ACE with a communal reading of "The Call of the First Disciples" in the Gospel of John. This is the famous passage where John the Baptist points out the still-enigmatic figure of Jesus, who is approaching in the distance.

Two disciples begin to follow, hesitantly interrupting the walking figure to ask him where he lives. Then Jesus utters his first, life-changing words, an invitation to discipleship: "Come and see" (Jn 1:39). After this reading, we ask our teachers to reflect personally and communally on this passage. We invite them to reflect on their own excitement and uncertainties about their decision to answer Christ's call to become teachers. And, taking our lead from John's gospel, we end with a question not about them, but about Christ: *What about Christ might have given the first disciples the ability to follow despite their uncertainties?* A journey toward deeper knowledge of Jesus has begun.

Later, after our participants share some of their first experiences as teachers, we read together Luke's account of Jesus' first teaching moment, unrolling the scroll of Isaiah in the synagogue at Nazareth. At first, struck by his authority, the crowd is rapt in awe. But in an instant, as Jesus' message changes from encouragement to stiff challenge, the same crowd prepares to throw him off the side of the town cliff. Our new teachers recognize this dynamic immediately from their own classroom experiences! They talk with increasing freedom and confidence about both the gospel passage and their own experiences with their students.

Again and again throughout their two-year formation—both as learners and as educators—they engage in this spiritual dynamic. When we read the gospels, we encounter Christ the Teacher. When we bring to the gospels the material of our daily lives, we seek to recognize the presence of Christ in our work as educators. One can sense throughout this process that a deep friendship is forming. Christ, like us, is a teacher and walks this journey intimately with us. Through this continual interpenetration of the gospels and our daily classroom experience, the two stories—of Christ the Teacher and of ourselves as teachers—begin to become one. Our lives as educators become a living out of the gospels.

After our graduation ceremony, when our teachers receive their master's degree diplomas, I make my way through the crowd of graduates and their proud families. As I encounter each one, I say something like, "You made it! How does it feel?" One year I said to a graduating teacher, "Congratulations! Do you feel smarter?" She had a more serious point to make. Standing in between her parents, her first teachers, she said, "I need you to know: what I most feel today is that I have come to know Jesus better. I am grateful for all of it, but that the most." It is from faith experiences and life experiences like these that this book is inspired and composed.

This book is written by a faith-filled community of educators—teachers, principals, administrators, and those who direct the formation of teachers and principals. There are many definitions of the Church. This book is a living witness to one of them: a community of believers reflecting on the Scriptures through the lens of their daily, lived experience, seeking to come to know more deeply Jesus Christ and how he continues to be present to them in their daily lives. Their short reflections should provide spiritual nourishment for any teacher trying to connect with Christ in the busyness of the school day.

We at ACE have come to know Christ the Teacher. And, as this book witnesses, we have come to love him and so seek to imitate him—indeed, to embody him, so that he may be known and loved again.

Fr. Lou DelFra, C.S.C.
Alliance for Catholic Education (ACE)
University of Notre Dame, Notre Dame, Indiana

REFLECTIONS

The Annunciation

Luke 1:26–28, 30–31, 34–38

In the sixth month the angel Gabriel was sent by God to a virgin whose name was Mary. And he came to her and said, "Do not be afraid, Mary, for you have found favor with God. And now, you will conceive in your womb and bear a son, and you will name him Jesus." Mary said to the angel, "How can this be, since I am a virgin?" The angel said to her, "The Holy Spirit will come upon you, and the power of the Most High will overshadow you; therefore the child to be born will be holy; he will be called Son of God. And now, your relative Elizabeth in her old age has also conceived a son; and this is the sixth month for her who was said to be barren. For nothing will be impossible with God." Then Mary said, "Here am I, the servant of the Lord; let it be with me according to your word." Then the angel departed from her.

It is likely that at one time or another, in our classrooms or in our lives, we have found ourselves wondering: *How can this be? How does this happen to me?* These words may fill our mind or escape our lips in times of profound grace or in moments of struggle. We cannot fathom our fortune or blessings at an unexpected breakthrough with a student, an unexpected answer to a problem, the opportunity to continue the work of Christ the Teacher (*How can this be?*). Or, we wrestle with deep frustration over failed efforts, things beyond our control, an unreachable student, a feeling of abandonment (*How does this happen to me?*).

In such moments Christ's first teacher, Mary, in her infinite grace and authenticity, becomes our teacher. When the angel announces that she is the chosen mother of Jesus, Mary does not get stuck in awe or confusion; she does not stop at the question, *How can this be?* Rather, her trust in God frees her to move forward with this powerful, enduring message: "My soul magnifies the Lord, and my spirit rejoices in God my Savior . . . for the Mighty One has done great things for me" (Lk 1:46, 49). In moments when we feel either blessed or worn down, we too can go beyond the question to find the answer, the heart of the message. We can refocus, renew, and remember to proclaim the greatness of the Lord—for indeed, he has done great things for each one of us.

PRAYER

Father, today help us remember the awe and the bewilderment we often share with Mary. And let us, with Mary, be moved to proclaim your greatness!

Kathleen Davidson, MEd
(Resurrection Catholic School, Pascagoula, MS)

The Visitation

Luke 1:39–42, 44

[After learning that she was pregnant by the Holy Spirit], Mary went with haste to the house of Zechariah and greeted Elizabeth. When Elizabeth heard Mary's greeting, the child leapt in her womb. And Elizabeth was filled with the Holy Spirit and exclaimed with a loud cry, "Blessed are you among women, and blessed is the fruit of your womb. As soon as I heard the sound of your greeting, the child in my womb leapt for joy."

Some teachers make it all look so effortless. Their charismatic presence alone can engage students and stir up excitement for learning. Their knowledge of their students and what motivates them seems downright mystical. They have the perfect explanation for everything, and can present the most difficult ideas to the most challenging students in such a way that the concept sticks forever. Their classrooms are organized and vibrant. Their grading is always done. Their students are happy and well behaved. Yes, it seems these teachers are the lucky few who were blessed with some elusive gift.

So what's your average, run-of-the-mill, trying-to-get-it-all-together teacher (like myself) to do after seeing such masters at work in the classroom? How tempting it is to feel inferior, to give up, to lament, "Why don't I have that gift?"

I wonder if John the Baptist felt this temptation. In many ways, the story of the Visitation begins a "tale of two teachers," with John, still in Elizabeth's womb, selflessly and exuberantly witnessing the presence of the Master Teacher before either was even born. Would John always feel this way? Would John feel inklings of inferiority as the boys grew up together? Would he grow weary later in life, with crowds asking constantly, "Are you the one?" (knowing that the answer was always "no")?

Perhaps the greatest testament to the teaching power of John is this: a truly awesome teacher would always find the humility, over and over, to say, "No, I am not he," and to continue leading people toward the true Christ, helping them recognize and choose to follow him. And that, of course, is the ultimate mission of any Christian school teacher—to help our students recognize, know, and follow Jesus.

The example of a gifted teacher is itself a gift to the rest of us teachers. May God grant each of us the grace to see such an example and, rather than falling victim to inferiority, affirm, "That's the teacher I want to be." May he grant us time with, and receptive minds and hearts toward, such master teachers, observing their ways and learning their secrets. When we fall short, may he give us the strength to get up and try again. And most especially, may our efforts, like John's, always show our students the way to Jesus.

PRAYER

Lord, help us to be humble students of Christ the Teacher, learning his ways and pointing others to the path of life.

Meghann Robinson Kirzeder, MEd
(St. Adalbert Catholic School, South Bend, IN)

MAGNIFICAT

LUKE 1:46–49

And Mary the mother of Christ said to Elizabeth,
"My soul magnifies the Lord,
and my spirit rejoices in God my Savior,
for he has looked with favor on the lowliness of his servant.
Surely, from now on all generations will call me blessed;
for the Mighty One has done great things for me,
and holy is his name."

In parallel stories in Luke's gospel, the Angel Gabriel announces miraculous births to Zechariah and Mary. Zechariah greets this news of Elizabeth's pregnancy with doubt, momentarily closed to God's message and therefore to the joy promised. To Mary, Gabriel announces something far more incredible. Mary's response to this mystery defines her as the first teacher of Christ.

The difference in their responses is subtle. Zechariah, realistic and grounded, asks, "How *can* this be?" There is doubt in his heart at the improbability of the promise. While Mary, in a far more confounding situation, responds, "How *will* this be?" And then, "I am the Lord's servant. Let it be done unto me as you have said." There is much magic in this moment. This is Mary's first act as a mother, as the first teacher of Jesus. As he enters her womb, she teaches him to respond to God's mystery with wonder, openness, and joy.

Mary does not understand, but she also does not doubt. Unlike Zechariah's initial response, she stands before mystery in *wonder*. Wonder is at the heart of education, which seeks to deepen our relationship with reality and with creation. As teachers, being people of wonder allows us to teach with wonder. Jesus is the perfect example of one full of wonder at God's goodness, and his ministry is defined by eliciting this wonder in others. "Now when Jesus had finished saying these things, the crowds were astounded at this teaching" (Mt 7:28).

Mary also responds with radical *openness* to the wonder of God's activity. Where Zechariah is initially closed, Mary is open like a child. Her "yes" is the first act of Christian discipleship, but also the first act of a great teacher. This "yes" in the face of mystery requires humility and faith. Zechariah is too bound to his preconceptions, his sense of control. Teaching requires a deep openness to what God has done, and will do. Christ is the perfect teacher because he is perfectly open to God's presence and will.

The results are striking. Zechariah is stricken dumb and cannot proclaim the joy that should be his. Mary's response is pure joy. She runs to Elizabeth and sings, "My soul glorifies the Lord and my spirit rejoices in God my Savior!"

The fruits of wonder and openness are the joy and peace of Christ the Teacher.

PRAYER

Lord, fill us with your Spirit so that we may be witnesses to wonder, and teachers of wonder, today.

TJ D'Agostino, MEd
(Charlotte Catholic High School, Charlotte, NC)

The Children of God

John 1:9–13

The true light, which enlightens everyone, was coming into the world. He was in the world, and the world came into being through him; yet the world did not know him. He came to what was his own, and his own people did not accept him. But to all who received him, who believed in his name, he gave power to become children of God, who were born, not of blood or of the will of the flesh or of the will of man, but of God.

I am a student. It's one of the few statements about me I can make with total certainty. I have been a student since my birth (learning how to breathe, eat, crawl, and walk), and I vow to be one until my exit out. I make this vow because the best teachers are always students, and I am also a teacher. I have been and continue to be a student-teacher. These are two great roles to play in this world.

One of the most profound lessons I have learned in this life is that even more than these two great things, I am this: a child of God. Thank God! And I thank God for the teachers and students who have helped me know this great truth—for at times, as a teacher and as a mom, it is easy to forget.

I ponder being a child of God particularly in moments when I am not feeling very confident: as a teacher, when the results of a test show the class never got it, and as a mother fumbling around in the newness of this role, searching for the master role models who can show me what it looks like when greatness mixes with this grand thing called motherhood. As a fledgling parent, former teacher, and forever student now raising two little boys under the age of three, I am slightly lacking in confidence and expertise, as most fledglings are. At times like these, I find myself tempted to ask, "Who am I?" without remembering the answer, "I am a child of God."

I need this reminder frequently, sometimes daily, sometimes moment by moment. This can be quite a feat since reflective moments can be hard to come by for classroom teachers or mothers of young children. But recently, all it took was a moment reading through some lovely letters from students of mine to remind me of the simply great answer to one of life's grandest questions. We (students, teachers, and parents) can find the truth if we look at each other and say, in one way or another, "You are a child of God!"

PRAYER

Lord, remind us that we are your children and that each person we encounter today is also your beloved child.

Emily Ludwikoski, MEd
(Saint Maria Goretti, Madison, WI)

The Word Became Flesh

John 1:14–18

And the Word became flesh and lived among us, and we have seen his glory, the glory as of a father's only son, full of grace and truth. (John testified to him and cried out, "This was he of whom I said, 'He who comes after me ranks ahead of me because he was before me.'") From his fullness we have all received grace upon grace. The law indeed was given through Moses; grace and truth came through Jesus Christ. No one has ever seen God. It is God the only Son, who is close to the Father's heart, who has made him known.

When we reflect on the lives of teachers, numerous daily and utterly human aspects typically come to mind. We think of busy school schedules, the endless stacks of papers to be graded, the noisy classrooms and hallways, and the sea of students' faces that pass through our classrooms day after day, year after year. Even when thinking of Christ as Teacher, we often focus on his human qualities as those we should aspire to embody: his inclusivity of children, his effective use of parables, and his ability to guide students to self-realized moments of enlightenment.

Yet, while we focus on the human challenges and rewards of teaching, Christ the Teacher reminds us also of the divinity inherent in teaching. We are doing *God's* work. We are the face of God on earth when we are in communion with our students, when we strive to see their potential as God does. When we teach, we are clearly human; we have struggles, hopes, and uncertainties. But we are also representatives of God. When we teach, we are called to glimpse the sacred mystery in each student. When we teach, eternal realities like truth and knowledge become real for our students, just as the Word and God's glory became real for Christ's students.

By teaching, in all its humanity, we gain a glimpse of the divine seed in each of us, which will one day be fully realized as we become one with the ultimate Truth, boundless Grace, and eternal Love.

PRAYER

Dear God, please help us recognize—and nurture—your presence in ourselves and our students.

Camille Fitzpatrick Markey, PhD
(Boston College, Chestnut Hill, MA)

Finding Jesus in the Temple

Luke 2:41–48, 51–52

Every year Jesus' parents went to Jerusalem for the Festival of the Passover. When he was twelve years old, they went up to the Festival, according to the custom. Afterwards, while his parents were returning home, the boy Jesus stayed behind in Jerusalem, but they were unaware of it. Then they began looking for him among their relatives and friends. When they did not find him, they went back to Jerusalem to look for him. After three days they found him in the temple courts, sitting among the teachers, listening to them and asking them questions. Everyone who heard him was amazed at his understanding and his answers. When his parents saw him, they were astonished. Then he went down to Nazareth with them and was obedient to them. But his mother treasured all these things in her heart. And as Jesus grew up, he increased in wisdom and in favor with God and people.

For twenty years, my parents have attended every single parent-teacher conference at our family's Catholic schools—regardless of our grades in each class. Though we Greene children have sometimes questioned this practice, we've always loved the support they gave us and our teachers, and we loved the stories they gleaned from those conferences! Some of the best ones came from meeting new teachers; invariably, Mom would begin: "Well, first of all, I have socks older than him!"

With this playful observation in mind, I turn to Luke's account of a young Jesus assuming his role as Christ the Teacher. Mary and Joseph are astonished to find Jesus in the Temple among the elders. Yet, my attention and heart are drawn to Jesus, who seems here to know that his Father has graced him with the gifts to teach, even before he "increased in wisdom and in favor with God and people."

After my first parent conferences as a new teacher, I called my mom to debrief her. I told stories about difficult but honest conversations, as well as encounters with parents who had come simply to offer support. When I finished, it took a few seconds before Mom responded.

Suddenly she was glimpsing the reality of her young daughter's position as a full-time teacher in a Christian school: a position worthy of respect, and one that required sufficient wisdom. Mom was utterly convinced of my ability to serve in this role (more convinced than I was, to be sure!), but she was also rendered speechless in realizing that her own daughter would not pass the "Sock Test."

Christian school teachers—especially new ones—can often find themselves in moments like these, when the role seems so great, the ministry so crucial, the responsibilities so overwhelming. May these teachers turn in prayer to the young Christ the Teacher, who by staying in close relationship with his Father, received a quiet assurance about his gifts as a teacher and responded generously to his call even before the world (and his mother!) thought he was ready.

PRAYER

Lord, keep us open to your will for us. Grant us the strength to respond to your call with enthusiastic, generous hearts.

Sarah Greene, MEd
(McGill-Toolen Catholic High School, Mobile, AL)

The Baptism of Jesus

Matthew 3:13–17

Then Jesus came from Galilee to the Jordan to be baptized by John. But John tried to deter him, saying, "I need to be baptized by you, and do you come to me?" Jesus replied, "Let it be so now; it is proper for us to do this to fulfill all righteousness." Then John consented. As soon as Jesus was baptized, he went up out of the water. At that moment heaven was opened, and he saw the Spirit of God descending like a dove and lighting on him. And a voice from heaven said, "This is my Son, whom I love; with him I am well pleased."

This is my Son, whom I love; with him I am well pleased." With these words, Jesus is publicly announced as God's beloved Son, and so begins his public ministry. In the same way, through our own Baptism we are publicly announced as Christians, sons and daughters of God whom he loves and with whom he is well pleased. These words lay the foundation of our ministry as teachers. As God loves us unconditionally, so we are called to love others.

When I was a young teacher, I remember the first time I saw my students as "my kids" *whom I love*. This occurred through an interaction with one of my fifth graders, Kevin.

Kevin wasn't the smartest or the most popular boy in the class, but he befriended everyone. If a classmate was alone at recess or lunch, Kevin was there with an invitation to join him. One week, he was acting strangely out of character and began getting in trouble during class. When I spoke with Kevin privately, I learned that his parents had a terrible argument and his mother had not been home for several days. Through my ministry as a teacher, he trusted in me and confided in me.

As a result, Kevin and I began meeting regularly before and after school. It was an easy sacrifice to make because I loved him. I embraced the fact that the role of a teacher includes that of mentor and parental figure. Looking back, I believe God gave me the grace to provide some stability, counsel, and love to Kevin during this tumultuous and insecure time in his life.

Each one of our students—and each of our coworkers, friends, relatives, and neighbors—is God's child, *whom God loves and with whom God is pleased.* It is from the recognition of this reality that our public ministry as teachers begins.

PRAYER

Father, thank you for the gift of our Baptism, which announces us as your children and commissions us as your witnesses. Help us to know and share the Father's love as Jesus did.

Matthew Moloney, MEd
(Holy Name Catholic School, Kansas City, KS)

The Temptation of Jesus

Matthew 4:1–11

Then Jesus was led by the Spirit into the wilderness to be tempted by the devil. He fasted, and afterwards he was famished. The tempter came and said to him, "If you are the Son of God, command these stones to become loaves of bread." But he answered, "It is written, 'One does not live by bread alone, but by every word that comes from the mouth of God.'" Then the devil placed him on the pinnacle of the temple, saying to him, "If you are the Son of God, throw yourself down." Jesus said to him, "Again it is written, 'Do not put the Lord your God to the test.'" Again, the devil took him to a very high mountain and showed him all the kingdoms of the world and their splendor; and he said to him, "All these I will give you, if you will fall down and worship me." Jesus said to him, "Away with you, Satan! For it is written, 'Worship the Lord your God, and serve only him.'" Then the devil left him, and suddenly angels came and waited on him.

Is this passage about Jesus the victor, who overcomes temptation to beat the devil at his own game? Or is it about Jesus the scholar, who quotes Scripture word for word in the face of peril? Or is it about Jesus the strong-willed, who demonstrates commendable fortitude when experiencing extreme physical discomfort and an opportunity to soothe the pangs of his human flesh? While all these designations may be fitting in one way or another, the hidden lesson to be found in this test comes from Christ the Teacher.

Jesus, having done his homework, knew that at some point he was going to have to face this situation. The worldly temptations of power and human satisfaction are simply too ubiquitous for anyone, even Jesus, to avoid for a lifetime. As such, the passage says he let himself be led into the forsaken desert for the sole purpose of being tempted. He willingly walked into a trying environment to confront his most difficult student: the one who got away. Christ the Teacher is the prepared instructor who leans heavily on his faith and holds his ground in even the most difficult of circumstances.

As educators, we know that there are often difficulties, sometimes of the highest sort, waiting for us. And we willingly walk into such environments, whether they are created by the words and behaviors of our students, their parents, or our own colleagues. A teacher's life is full of these challenges, and we can be tempted to take the easy way out. We can give in to bitterness, paybacks, or even resigned indifference.

Christ the Teacher, in the passage of the temptation in the desert, shows us a different way. He calls us to prepare; to know the challenges we will face; and especially to rely on God's strength when our students, our classes, or our environments put us to the test.

PRAYER

Jesus, help us lean on our faith in you today so that we can hold our ground in even the most difficult of circumstances.

Ricky Austin, MEd
(St. Hilary School, Chicago, IL)

Jesus Is the Lamb of God

John 1:29–31

The next day he saw Jesus coming towards him and declared, "Here is the Lamb of God who takes away the sin of the world! This is he of whom I said, 'After me comes a man who ranks ahead of me because he was before me.' I myself did not know him; but I came baptizing with water for this reason, that he might be revealed to Israel."

As a new teacher, when my students misbehaved I wrote their names on the board. If they did not correct the behavior, they had to complete a behavior form describing what they did wrong. At parent-teacher conferences, they shared this form with their parents. I would see them squirm in their seats as they tried to explain the reason for their misbehavior confessed in their own handwriting. Inside, I was squirming too. During these meetings, and when I would erase the board at the end of each day, I would think of these struggling students and feel demoralized.

One evening at prayer, I read John the Baptist's words when he first saw Jesus, "Here is the Lamb of God who takes away the sins of the world!" (Jn 1:29). I began to consider this more deeply. What if I said this in my classroom? Would my students be inspired to do as John's pupils did and follow the Christ? Is that not our goal as Christian educators? The more I thought about this, the more my strategy for handling problem behavior came to mind. What difference would it make if I shifted gears and concentrated on the good behaviors of my students? If I focused on the good, and then said, "Here is the Lamb of God!" would my students respond?

The next day I shared my thoughts with my students. I said that because I wanted them to experience God, I felt compelled to change. Instead of putting the names of the misbehaving students on the board, I would write the names of the students who were behaving well. Half the class celebrated. No more than ten minutes later in the first lesson, I was writing the names of my well-behaved students on the board. Only fifteen minutes into this new approach, I stopped writing on the board, turned around, and said to my class, "Wow, look at all the great students I have." I could see in their faces that the students felt better about themselves, and I know I felt better about them too. I learned that day a powerful lesson about how to draw others closer to the Lamb of God.

PRAYER

Lord, through our teaching, may all students come to know and follow you.

Keiran Roche, MEd
(Santa Cruz Catholic School, Tucson, AZ)

Jesus' First Disciples

John 1:35–39

The next day John the Baptist again was standing with two of his disciples, and as he watched Jesus walk by, he exclaimed, "Look, here is the Lamb of God!" The two disciples heard him say this, and they followed Jesus. When Jesus turned and saw them following, he said to them, "What are you looking for?" They said to him, "Rabbi (which translated means Teacher), where are you staying?" He said to them, "Come and see." They came and saw where he was staying, and they remained with him that day. It was about four o'clock in the afternoon.

There must have been something powerfully alluring about Jesus. At a word from him, people left their work, their possessions, even their families to follow him. For any teacher who has struggled to hold his or her students' attention for even a fifty-minute period, this ability of Jesus is nothing short of a miracle! How did he do it?

Jesus does not begin with the Ten Commandments, nor lecture his new followers about the long history of humanity's shortcomings, nor provide an exhaustive list of what will be required of them if they are to enter into eternal life with him. Jesus knows all these things to be important and that his followers will eventually need to understand them in order to be truly happy, but he also intuits that these are not what they need to know initially. What they need is to answer what Jesus asks first: "What are you looking for?" Even when their response reveals that they respect Jesus' authority as Teacher, still he does not use that authority to bend them to his will—benevolent though it is—or force the answer upon them. Rather, he extends an invitation for them to share what is his: "Come, and you will see."

It is a constant temptation for us teachers—along with just about everyone else—to mold others to our own intentions. Whether or not those intentions are altruistic, we fall short of Jesus' example as long as we view other people through the lens of our own agenda rather than theirs. Students—indeed all people—are not objects to be manipulated or projects to be completed. They are individuals to be engaged in the context of relationship.

In whatever role we find ourselves—students or teachers, employees or employers, children or parents—we are called as Christians not to be legislators of truth, but bearers of a promise. The greatest gift we can offer others is an invitation to join us on the journey in which we ourselves daily struggle and rejoice—the journey to come and see where Christ lives. Such was the pedagogy of Jesus, whom we seek to emulate—if not because he is the Teacher *par excellence*, then certainly because he somehow managed to get students to follow after him at four in the afternoon.

PRAYER

Lord, be ever at our side as we journey with our students in the way you have shown us.

Patrick Manning, MEd, MTS
(Bishop Byrne High School, Memphis, TN)

Jesus Calls Peter, James, and John

Luke 5:3–6, 8–10

Jesus got into the boat belonging to Simon. [Then] he said to Simon, "Put out into the deep water and let down your nets for a catch." Simon answered, "Master, we have worked all night long but have caught nothing. Yet if you say so, I will let down the nets." When they had done this, they caught so many fish that their nets were beginning to break. When Simon Peter saw it, he fell down at Jesus' knees, saying, "Go away from me, Lord, for I am a sinful man!" For he and all who were with him were amazed at the catch of fish that they had taken; and so also were James and John, sons of Zebedee, who were partners with Simon. Then Jesus said to Simon, "Do not be afraid; from now on you will be catching people."

In this passage Simon Peter, with his resigned acceptance of Jesus' command, assumes that Jesus is ignorant of the disciples' prior, failed fishing trip. He thinks that Jesus does not see his shortcomings, and he doubts that Jesus' directive will prove fruitful. The same mantra of self-doubt is repeated throughout the

Bible. Moses says, "O my Lord, I have never been eloquent . . . but I am slow of speech and slow of tongue" (Ex 4:10). Isaiah wails, "Woe is me! I am lost, for I am a man of unclean lips . . ." (Is 6:5). Paul sighs, "For I am the least of the apostles, unfit to be called an apostle" (1 Cor 15:9).

These insecurities and failings are familiar territory for educators. We often recognize them in our students. This student won't read aloud. That student won't attempt a new math problem. We also see them in ourselves. As Christian educators we are called to numerous roles. We can't possibly fill every one perfectly; and so our limitations and insecurities surface.

But as with Isaiah, Moses, Paul, and Simon Peter, Christ the Teacher pushes us past our defeats and deficiencies with a simple command: "Do not be afraid; from now on you will be catching people." In other words, *Follow me—I have a job for you!* Christ the Teacher does not condemn our inadequacies, but allows us the chance to rise above them. He trusts us, despite everything. And through this trust, Christ gives our failures dignity, and our limitations purpose.

Christ the Teacher's confidence in us transcends our imperfections, and so as Christian educators, we can learn to trust ourselves to the precious mission Christ has laid out before us.

PRAYER

Christ our Teacher, let us push out to deep water today and cast our nets again, remembering with comfort and hope your words: "Do not be afraid."

Laura MacLean, MEd
(San Juan Diego Catholic High School, Austin, TX)

Jesus Teaches Nicodemus

John 3:1–5

Now there was a Pharisee named Nicodemus, a leader of the Jews. He came to Jesus by night and said to him, "Rabbi, we know that you are a teacher who has come from God; for no one can do these signs that you do apart from the presence of God." Jesus answered him, "Very truly, I tell you, no one can see the kingdom of God without being born from above." Nicodemus said to him, "How can anyone be born after having grown old? Can one enter a second time into the mother's womb and be born?" Jesus answered, "Very truly, I tell you, no one can enter the kingdom of God without being born of water and Spirit."

M*y students will find out that I don't know everything.* That was the stomach-twisting worry keeping me up nights during my first months of teaching. During French class, I was astounded by the specific and often bizarre vocabulary my students wanted to know, asking me, for example, "Miss Blair, how do you say *porcupine* in French?" "That is why you have a dictionary," I would respond as a way of skirting the question so I could consult my own dictionary later. After all, now that I was a teacher, wasn't I supposed to know all the answers?

Nicodemus did not admit that he didn't know whether Jesus was really the Son of God. This teacher snuck away at night to ask *the* Teacher questions, but he never shared his doubts. Of course, Jesus knew the truth and loved Nicodemus for coming to him anyway, just as he loves us in whatever state we come to him—confused and searching for answers, or enlightened and praising him with thanks. It would be a huge mistake for me to believe I should always have all the answers to my students' questions, just as it would be a mistake to think I should have all the answers to my own. God allows us times of not knowing, perhaps precisely so that we may ask Jesus to show us the way. He allows us times of doubt so that we can admit to others, and to our God, "I don't know." With confusion comes humility that draws us closer to him.

In such moments may we approach Jesus as Nicodemus did, secure in knowing that, no matter our state of mind, God loves us as we are.

PRAYER

Loving Savior, let us find comfort in you, whether we are struggling with doubts or are filled with certainty.

Michelle Blair Fuller, MEd
(Bishop Kenny High School, Jacksonville, FL)

Jesus' Teaching on Love

John 3:16

For God so loved the world that he gave his only Son, so that everyone who believes in him may not perish but may have eternal life.

Educators are fond of definitions. We look them up, write them out, and commit them to memory. Definitions help us to understand, providing nuance to our speech and guidance for our word selection. If a correct definition is known and available, the chances of clear communication and decisive action markedly increase.

Dictionaries and other reference works are the most common places to look up a definition. Most people would never look to the Bible for a definition or consult the gospels for clarification about a particular word. But some passages of Scripture sound like definitions, attempts at clarifying a concept with multiple meanings. John 3:16, an often-quoted gospel passage, points us in the direction of a definition: "God so loved the world that he gave his only Son, so that everyone who believes in him might not perish but have eternal life." The Gospel indicates that love, flowing from God, made present in the person of Jesus, is the redeeming grace central to the universe.

Have you ever wondered what the definition of love is? Surely, this is a question swirling deep in the hearts and minds of our students. Another Scripture verse says, "In this is love, not that we loved God but that he loved us and sent his only Son into the world so that we might live through him" (1 Jn 4:10). The first and primary definition of love is that love is of God and comes from God. Love is not primarily about us or what we do or how we feel. Love begins with God's love for us. We love only because we have first been loved by God.

And in case that definition is not clear, Scripture follows up with an even more precise definition—not for love, but for God. The definition: "God is love." God does not have love, or bestow love, or even create love. No, God is love. Upon these definitions rests our understanding of who God is and why we, created in God's likeness, care so deeply for one another.

PRAYER

O God, who is Love, help us to stay ever mindful that love is our origin, our constant calling, and our fulfillment in heaven.

Fr. Ron Nuzzi, PhD
(University of Notre Dame, Notre Dame, IN)

Jesus Talks with a Samaritan Woman

John 4:6–7, 9–11, 16–18, 28–29

Jesus came to a Samaritan city and, tired out by his journey, was sitting by a well. It was about noon. A Samaritan woman came to draw water, and Jesus said to her, "Give me a drink." The Samaritan woman said to him, "How is it that you, a Jew, ask a drink of me, a woman of Samaria?" (Jews do not share things in common with Samaritans.) Jesus answered her, "If you knew the gift of God, and who it is that is saying to you, 'Give me a drink,' you would have asked him, and he would have given you living water." The woman said to him, "Sir, you have no bucket, and the well is deep. Where do you get that living water?" Jesus said to her, "Go, call your husband, and come back." The woman answered him, "I have no husband." Jesus said to her, "You are right in saying, 'I have no husband;' for you have had five husbands, and the one you have now is not your husband. What you have said is true!" Then the woman left her water jar and went back to the city. She said to the people, "Come and see a man who told me everything I have ever done!"

Throughout the gospels, Jesus often interacts with those who are mired in sin and most in need of his presence. Nowhere is this more pronounced than in this story about Jesus with the woman at the well. The interaction between Jesus and the woman, although brief, epitomizes the transformative powers of Christ the Teacher. Although he is aware of the woman's apparent limitations, Jesus sees beyond them to someone who is in need of transformation through his compassion and trust. Before her encounter with Christ, the Samaritan was burdened with feelings of inadequacies. Ashamed of her sins, she avoided others by going to the well at noon, the hottest and therefore least frequented time of the day. Through the relationship she finds in Christ, however, the Samaritan is transformed into a disciple who can now confidently proclaim the Good News of Jesus.

Like Christ's interaction with the Samaritan woman, Christian educators are called to transform students by forming relationships based on compassion and trust. Rather than seeing just a sinful woman, Christ the Teacher shows compassion for her and teaches her. Rather than avoiding the Samaritan, Christ welcomes the encounter and shows faith in her when he reveals himself as the Messiah.

Students who are most in need of a transformative relationship from a teacher are often those who, like the Samaritan woman, "deserve" it the least. As imitators of Christ, Christian teachers recognize this and look beneath the surface to acknowledge the potential of all students.

PRAYER

Holy Redeemer, by your grace, give us your eyes that we may see the heart of every student we serve.

Patrick Flanagan, MEd
(St. Rita Catholic School, Rockford, IL)

The Appointing of the Twelve Apostles

Mark 3:13–19

Jesus went up the mountain and called to him those whom he wanted, and they came to him. And he appointed twelve, whom he also named apostles, to be with him, and to be sent out to proclaim the message, and to have authority to cast out demons. So he appointed the Twelve: Simon (to whom he gave the name Peter); James son of Zebedee and John the brother of James (to whom he gave the name Boanerges, that is, Sons of Thunder); and Andrew, and Philip, and Bartholomew, and Matthew, and Thomas, and James son of Alphaeus, and Thaddaeus, and Simon the Cananaean and Judas Iscariot, who betrayed him.

Christ chose some rough-and-tumble members for his apostolic crew. Among the Twelve were James and John, brothers whom Jesus nicknamed *Sons of Thunder*. One can imagine how they earned the name; one can imagine Christ's patience as he molded them into men of God. When our patience is tried by the more raucous members of our own classrooms, it is helpful to remember that the Teacher did not call already-perfect students, but those who would love him and persevere in his will. James was the first apostle to be martyred. It was John to whom Jesus entrusted the Blessed Mother.

I once taught a son of thunder. His personality was too great for a desk and chair. He was brilliant and refused to show his work. His shirt was smudged with food, and his class binder was a disaster. While I gave notes, he would cross his eyes by staring at the tip of his pencil. He had a habit of telling me silly stories during those frenzied times when it's all you can do to keep five things straight in your head and make it to lunch without a student telling you a silly story.

The second year I taught him, he was removed from his home because of a neglectful mother. It was then I saw that his thunder was just a cry to be seen, loved, and even disciplined. Later that year I received a handwritten certificate and a cheap calendar from his tutoring service. The certificate said "Favorite Teacher Award." I nearly wept. I am not sure I ever got him to show his work, but I think together we learned to love.

PRAYER

Lord Jesus, for all the sons and daughters of thunder among us, fill us with your compassion and grace.

Barbara Jane Sloan, MEd
(Holy Spirit Preparatory School, Atlanta, GA)

Light of the World to Others

Matthew 5:1–9, 14, 16

When Jesus saw the crowds, he went up the mountain. Then he began to speak, saying: "Blessed are the poor in spirit, for theirs is the kingdom of heaven. Blessed are those who mourn, for they will be comforted. Blessed are the meek, for they will inherit the earth. Blessed are those who hunger and thirst for righteousness, for they will be filled. Blessed are the merciful, for they will receive mercy. Blessed are the pure in heart, for they will see God. Blessed are the peacemakers, for they will be called children of God. You are the light of the world. Let your light shine before others, so that they may see your good works and give glory to your Father in heaven."

In the Sermon on the Mount, where we find this passage, Jesus seems to say all kinds of crazy things, like "blessed are the poor" and "blessed are those who mourn, for they will be comforted." Then, not content to stop there, he says to these poor and mournful people, "You are the light of the world."

In the fifth-grade classroom where I once taught, this is emblazoned across the wall. *You are the light of the world.* Our children need to see that; they need to learn it to their core so they remember who they are and show it boldly. Even in my work now with college students, I've found this lesson of Jesus is essential to their sense of self. It expresses so much of what Jesus' own light-filled life embodied: his healings; his condemnation of the Sadducees and Pharisees; his intentional friendships with those on the margins; the offering of himself on the cross; and his constant reminder that he is with us, *in* us, in the Eucharist. Jesus was always doing this deep, look-you-in-the-eye, turn-it-back-to-you teaching. *Your* faith has saved you, trust *your* inner authority, blessed are *you*.

You are the light of the world. This is Jesus' teaching for us, his students. He asks us to radically reclaim who we are in God's kingdom and live this lesson boldly in our lives. Likewise, he calls us as teachers to model this same seemingly upside-down, authoritative teaching to our children and to one another and to give each other permission to live confident, radiant, uniquely light-filled lives.

PRAYER

Jesus our Savior, give us the humility to hear you when you say, "You are the light of the world," and the freedom to be who we are.

Erin Duffy, MEd
(Our Lady of Perpetual Help School, Dallas, TX)

Light of the World on Us

Matthew 5:13–16

And Jesus said, "You are the salt of the earth; but if salt has lost its taste, how can its saltiness be restored? It is no longer good for anything, but is thrown out and trampled underfoot. You are the light of the world. A city built on a hill cannot be hidden. No one after lighting a lamp puts it under the bushel basket, but on the lamp stand, and it gives light to all in the house. In the same way, let your light shine before others, so that they may see your good works and give glory to your Father in heaven."

Like many of us who are called to the field of Christian education, I took this mandate seriously when I put aside other career opportunities to serve in low-income schools and perhaps provide a little saving grace for students in need. I began my training with head held high, ready to let my "light shine before others, that they may see your good deeds and give glory to God." Little did I know that I would soon find myself in the darkness needing others to shine Christ's light on me.

By the time I started teaching, I found I had little light to give. My mother had died suddenly six months prior to my first classroom assignment. My faith had been badly shaken, and my spirit overtaken with grief.

Gradually, however, I was able to see the light of Christ as it persistently shone through the faces of the students I was sent to serve. It shone through a handmade card thanking me for being a teacher, a banner that welcomed me back after I ran a marathon, the students who visited me long after their time in my class, and the single rose in a vase placed on my desk for May Day. Slowly, these acts of "light" restored my ability to glorify God. Unexpectedly, these students had become Christ the Teacher for me!

Christ has called all of his disciples to "let their light shine before others." Surely that call is made powerfully to us as teachers. But may we not forget that our students have received that same call too, and the glory of God is often revealed to us in them.

PRAYER

Light of the World, thank you for shining your light on us in unexpected ways. Help us to reflect that light today.

Ellen Riley, MEd
(St. Michael the Archangel, Leawood, KS)

Love Your Enemies

Luke 6:27–31

Jesus said, "I say to you who listen, love your enemies, do good to those who hate you, bless those who curse you, pray for those who abuse you. If anyone strikes you on the cheek, offer the other also; and from anyone who takes away your coat do not withhold even your shirt. Give to everyone who begs from you; and if anyone takes away your goods, do not ask for them again. Do to others as you would have them do to you."

We tend to assume that Jesus was a pretty skilled craftsman, but a glimpse into his carpentry shop might reveal some surprises. Imagine Christ trying to use a saw to pound in a nail or a hammer to sand down the top of a table.

That's what we might expect after hearing Jesus preach, because he asks us to use powerful tools in very strange ways. We are to develop vulnerability, and present it to those who harm; to cultivate generosity, and spend it on those who steal; to nurture love, and place it at the feet of enemies. Essentially, Jesus invites us to develop exceptional virtues, only to waste them extravagantly. He pushes us to excellence, but excellence in service of goals that appear unworthy. As teacher, Christ gives us a new rubric for measuring success.

Christian educators are charged with doing the same. We help our students develop the skills that the world demands, but we instill in them a desire to use that education in ways that the world often derides. Though we give them the tools to earn power and wealth, we teach them to be with and to serve the weak and the poor. Though we give them the tools to outperform their competition, we teach them to prize others' success above their own. Though we give them the tools to be leaders, we teach them to be servants. We remember that for Christ, the skills are important, but it's the criteria on the rubric that make all the difference.

PRAYER

God of mercy, guide the use of our gifts, and shape our understanding of success.

Stephen Calme, MEd
(St. Joseph Academy, St. Augustine, FL)

Giving to the Needy

Matthew 6:1–4

And Jesus said, "Beware of practicing your piety before others in order to be seen by them; for then you have no reward from your Father in heaven. So whenever you give alms, do not sound a trumpet before you, as the hypocrites do in the synagogues and in the streets, so that they may be praised by others. Truly I tell you, they have received their reward. But when you give alms, do not let your left hand know what your right hand is doing, so that your alms may be done in secret; and your Father who sees in secret will reward you."

To teach, in large measure, is to struggle—with curricula, with demanding students, with the rigor of a profession that, if we are to believe the news, is both the cause of and solution to all of society's problems. No pressure.

The cruelest turn, of course, in so draining a professional life is that many of the rewards of a teacher are deferred—and so our good work is hidden. Students will come back years or even decades later, grown versions of the children we once knew, full of thanks for a kind word, a safe classroom, a chance embrace in the midst of a dark time; and oh the joy to have made a difference! But what is one to do in the midst of the detritus of crashed online grade books, fidgety February sixth graders, and one more accreditation meeting? It is not easy to "give in secret," as the Lord commanded.

St. Francis of Assisi, in his tonsured wisdom (bedecked with birds and squirrels, a man who perhaps never had the pleasure of grade checks before Friday athletic contests) granted teachers this advice about giving in secret: "Preach the Gospel at all times and when necessary use words."

Our students have great and many needs. When we are at our best, solving all of the little dilemmas that make up an assembly day in the middle of a week, we are preaching away—but most often in secret with no trumpets in earshot. So it is that our students come back to us in our later lives, physically or perhaps only in spirit, secretly. Their growth and formation are our often-quiet reward for a life well taught, a teaching day subtly preached, not in words but in the caring actions of our daily lives as teachers.

PRAYER

We pray, Lord, with left hand and right, that you make us secret trumpets of your Gospel every day.

Kevin Burke, PhD
(University of Notre Dame, Notre Dame, IN)

Rest for the Weary

Matthew 11:28–30

At that time, Jesus said, "All things have been handed over to me by my Father; and no one knows the Son except the Father, and no one knows the Father except the Son and anyone to whom the Son chooses to reveal him. Come to me, all you who are weary and are carrying heavy burdens and I will give you rest. Take my yoke upon you, and learn from me; for I am gentle and humble in heart, and you will find rest for your souls. For my yoke is easy, and my burden is light."

I am continually struck by the yokes that lie across the shoulders of so many of our students. A high school student once confided in me that he was a recovering alcoholic and drug addict. I became his confidant at school as he journeyed through sobriety. He told me about his struggles and fears. When he turned to the Lord for serenity, courage, and wisdom, this young man experienced a powerful conversion. I witnessed in him the lightness that comes from exchanging our yokes for the yoke of Christ.

He was always very spiritual, yet he continued to grow in his faith as he prepared for his Confirmation.

I knew he was anxious about selecting a saint name, so in one of our many spiritual discussions, I shared with him my favorite quote from St. Augustine: "Our hearts are restless, O Lord, until they rest in thee."

My student and I agreed that we could relate to these words, as we could to St. Augustine himself. We loved the dynamic between Augustine and his mother, Monica, because their relationship in faith shows the incredible power of prayer. We appreciated the fact that, even though his conversion came later in life, Augustine was able to teach and make a difference in the lives of so many people largely because of the struggles he overcame with God's grace. Augustine teaches us that we can turn to God even when we think *it's too late.* My student teaches us that Christ's response is a yoke that is light, lifting our burden, giving us serenity in our restlessness.

At the end of the school year, my student chose Augustine as his Confirmation saint. A few months later, I attended his Alcoholics Anonymous (AA) meeting when he received his one-year chip. Today, he remains sober because his once-restless heart has found its rest in God.

PRAYER

Lord, lift our burdens and help our hearts to rest in you.

Stephanie Kersting, MEd
(St. Michael the Archangel High School, Baton Rouge, LA)

The Parable of the Weeds

Matthew 13:24–30

Jesus told them another parable: "The kingdom of heaven may be compared to someone who sowed good seed in his field; but while everybody was asleep, an enemy came and sowed weeds among the wheat, and then went away. So when the plants came up and bore grain, then the weeds appeared as well. And the slaves of the householder came and said to him, 'Master, did you not sow good seed in your field? Where, then, did these weeds come from?' He answered, 'An enemy has done this.' The slaves said to him, 'Then do you want us to go and gather them?' But he replied, 'No, for in gathering the weeds you would uproot the wheat along with them. Let both of them grow together until the harvest; and at harvest time I will tell the reapers: Collect the weeds first and bind them in bundles to be burned, but gather the wheat into my barn.'"

I once asked my sixth graders, "What is the kingdom of God like?" Some drew thrones, others puppies; some described emotions of joy, and others wrote poems about angels.

But amid such wonderfully sentimental and otherworldly images, a deeper question arises: What is the kingdom of God like here and now, in the complexity of our world today? In this world, as this parable and experience tell us, Christ sows his field with disciples like you and me. At the same time, the Enemy is sowing seeds in the very same field—seeds of temptation, hatred, injustice. We must grow alongside these weeds, indeed in the midst of them, if we wish to build up the kingdom.

Here, Christ the Teacher provides us with a lesson on judgment, for how easy it is to judge the weeds among us rather than to grow patiently alongside them, slowly transforming the garden. God sows us as disciples, not as judges. We are called to be God's body on earth, building his kingdom of peace and love. When we take it upon ourselves to cast judgment, we inevitably uproot the wheat among the weeds.

How often do we adopt the gossip in the faculty room? How often do we evaluate students based on their parents, or on only their worst behavior? On what basis do we decide who may enroll in our schools or learn in our classrooms?

We can be the wheat that bears the fruit, but only if we are willing to be planted among some apparent weeds, patiently cooperating in God's transformation of the whole field. With Christ's strength, patience, and compassion, we can build God's kingdom on earth, starting in our own classrooms and communities.

PRAYER

Our transforming God, sow us as your disciples. Lead us away from judgment, and change us to see the world as you do: with compassion and understanding.

Kathryn DiPietro Hnatiuk, MEd
(Holy Angels School, Arcadia, CA)

Jesus and the Woman with a Hemorrhage

Luke 8:43–48

Now there was a woman who had been suffering from hemorrhages for twelve years; and though she had spent all she had on physicians, no one could cure her. She came up behind him and touched the fringe of his clothes, and immediately her hemorrhage stopped. Then Jesus asked, "Who touched me?" When all denied it, Peter said, "Master, the crowds surround you and press in on you." But Jesus said, "Someone touched me; for I noticed that power had gone out from me." When the woman saw that she could not remain hidden, she came trembling; and falling down before him, she declared in the presence of all the people why she had touched him, and how she had been immediately healed. He said to her, "Daughter, your faith has made you well; go in peace."

She was nameless, destitute, and isolated from her own community. Her condition made her unclean, and anyone who touched her became unclean. The woman with a hemorrhage spent twelve years desperately sinking all of her money into physicians who could not cure her. And so as she approached Jesus that day, the crowd silently avoided contact with her, an irritating obstacle in their path as they followed Jesus to the home of an important synagogue official. Using this to her advantage, she surreptitiously reached out for the tassel of Jesus' cloak and found herself cured.

Jesus could have let her slip away, content to have stopped her bleeding. Yet, she needed more than physical healing; she needed to be restored to the community, her dignity reclaimed.

Jesus made a big production out of "looking" for the person who touched his cloak. When she came forward and shared her story, Jesus lifted her and her story up as a model of faith for all gathered there. Her former "uncleanness" and shame prevented her from full participation in society. Now wholeness and dignity enabled her to find belonging and a meaningful place in her community.

Who are the students isolated from their peers? Who are the "untouchables" walking the halls in loneliness? Do we see when they silently reach out for help? How can we help restore their dignity? How can we help them and others see their wholeness and value? How can we, in imitation of Christ the

Teacher, help them find a sense of belonging in our community?

PRAYER

Christ, be in our eyes today, so we may see the invisible and downtrodden and recognize the worth and dignity of each life that surrounds us.

Jessica Ovel Hull, MAT
(Notre Dame de Sion High School, Kansas City, MO)

Jesus Calms the Sea

Matthew 8:23–27

And when Jesus got into the boat, his disciples followed him. A gale arose on the lake, so great that the boat was being swamped by the waves; but he was asleep. And they went and woke him up, saying, "Lord, save us! We are perishing!" And he said to them, "Why are you afraid, you of little faith?" Then he got up and rebuked the winds and the sea; and there was a dead calm. They were amazed, saying, "What sort of man is this, that even the winds and the sea obey him?"

The story of Jesus calming the sea is rich with lessons for how to be a compassionate teacher. Foremost among them, a teacher leads by getting in the boat first, even if the seas appear somewhat choppy, and then inviting the students to come aboard. Learning is by definition stressful and stormy, for it is a conflict between what is known and what is to be learned. Teachers invite their students to stretch beyond the comfortable known in order to experience novel concepts, skills, or ways of understanding themselves and the world.

Being challenged intellectually, emotionally, or spiritually can be exciting, but it can also be frightening. Anxiety is a normal human response to such challenges, and it can be helpful in the learning process as it sharpens attention and motivates action. But when anxiety involves too much unease, it can leave children feeling alone and overwhelmed by fear.

Christ's actions in the boat remind us that a teacher is called to be a compassionate facilitator and guide through times of stress. Christ's challenge for the disciples to have faith suggests that teachers are more effective when they encourage students to believe in themselves and to remember that they are safe in the learning environment. The teacher helps calm students by believing in them, thus providing a new way to face challenges in life—that is, with courage and faith. Thus, teaching means not only challenging students to grow, but also encouraging them to believe that with God they have what it takes to calm the storms that naturally arise within.

PRAYER

Lord, help us not to fear but to put our trust in you. Be with us always as we try to live out your love in all that we do.

Erik Goldschmidt, PhD (Boston College, Boston, MA)
Tiffany Carter, MA (Elberta Middle School, Elberta, AL)
Elise Taylor, Age 11 (St. Benedict School, Elberta, AL)

Jesus Rebukes the Wind

Mark 4:35–41

On that day, when evening had come, Jesus said to them, "Let us go across to the other side." And leaving the crowd behind, they took him with them in the boat, just as he was. Other boats were with him. A great gale arose, and the waves beat into the boat, so that the boat was already being swamped. But he was in the stern, asleep on a cushion; and they woke him up and said to him, "Teacher, do you not care that we are perishing?" He woke up and rebuked the wind, and said to the sea, "Peace! Be still!" Then the wind ceased, and there was a dead calm. He said to them, "Why are you afraid? Have you still no faith?" And they were filled with great awe and said to one another, "Who then is this, that even the wind and the sea obey him?"

When I pray with this gospel passage, I am struck by the "tough love" Jesus shows not merely to his disciples, but to his Father's creation—the wind and the sea! He is strong. He is forceful. He is in control. And the wind and the waves obey him. This passage reminds me of a great teacher in my life who taught as Jesus did.

Sister Bernadette McNamara was a tiny, Irish sister. She moved to the United States forty years ago and was the principal of St. Peter the Apostle School in Pascagoula, Mississippi. St. Peter's served a population of low-income students. The school was her baby, and the students were her "babes." She had the largest heart for them. She gave her life to them.

Sister ran a tight ship at St. Peter's. Everything was "Yes, Sister" or "No, Sister." The reason for all of this was structure. The children needed structure in their hectic lives. When the students were in school, they knew what to expect. And, more importantly, they knew that they were loved.

This love was not always warm and fuzzy. Sister showed the children tough love. She had high expectations, and if they weren't met, it was known. One afternoon, as I stood talking to Sister in the after-school daycare room, one of the five-year-old students behind her hurled a crayon across the room. After forty years, Sister had fully developed eyes on the back of her head! She whirled around, forcefully put her hand down on the desk, and said, "We do not act that way." The student said, "Yes, Sister." I will never forget that image: the look of surprise on the student's face coupled with the image of respect and love the moment Sister locked eyes with him. I think I know what the wind and sea felt like that day Jesus rebuked them. I highly doubt that student threw a crayon again.

Sister was my first experience as a teacher of the power of tough love. A teacher's love always means "I am with you; I am for you—unconditionally." To teach as Jesus did is to love powerfully and unconditionally.

PRAYER

We desire, loving Father, the grace to teach as Jesus did, and to love our students unconditionally.

Elizabeth Stowe Fennell, MEd
(Newton Country Day School of the Sacred Heart, Newton, MA)

Jesus Quiets the Storm

Luke 8:22–25

One day Jesus got into a boat with his disciples, and he said to them, "Let us go across to the other side of the lake." So they put out, and while they were sailing he fell asleep. A gale swept down on the lake, and the boat was filling with water, and they were in danger. They went to him and woke him up, shouting, "Master, Master, we are perishing!" And he woke up and rebuked the wind and the raging waves; they ceased, and there was a calm. He said to them, "Where is your faith?" They were afraid and amazed, and said to one another, "Who then is this, that he commands even the winds and the water, and they obey him?"

What strikes me about this passage is that a group of experienced fishermen was so scared of a squall that they had to wake the carpenter in search of solace. They must have weathered storms before. Where was the confidence one would assume veteran fishermen would have in the face of a storm?

When I was teaching middle school, I'd often spend a few days before a test helping my students put together a review sheet. Often, early in the activity, the students would start to complain that there was too much information, that there was no way they would remember all the facts for the test. I would remind them that they had already learned the material and that reviewing well would show them how much they really knew. It boiled down to confidence in their ability to demonstrate on the test what they already knew. And my role as a teacher was to show them that I was confident in them so that they could forge ahead.

Jesus displays this loving confidence in this passage. His taking a nap during a storm is evidence that he has confidence in his disciples' sailing abilities. But like our students, the disciples are quick to lose confidence and look to Jesus for help. When he asks, "Why are you terrified? Do you not have faith?" perhaps he is really asking them why they don't have faith, not only in him, but in their own abilities as frequent sailors of the sea.

Students in today's society often need someone to have confidence in them. Sometimes, somewhat unfortunately, the only people who can do this are their teachers. Let us look to Jesus—who looked lovingly on his disciples caught in a squall and invited them to trust in him and in themselves—as our example in seeing the abilities in each student we serve.

PRAYER

You, oh Lord, are the giver of all good gifts. Instill in us the confidence to use our gifts to do your will in the world.

Patrick Fennessy, MEd, MA
(St. Joseph School, Seattle, WA)

The Disciples Question Jesus

Mark 7:14–18

Then Jesus called the crowd again and said to them, "Listen to me, all of you, and understand: there is nothing outside a person that by going in can defile, but the things that come out are what defile." When he had left the crowd and entered the house, his disciples asked him about the parable. He said to them, "Then do you also fail to understand?"

The disciples were undoubtedly the first recipients of a Christian education. Yet even from their privileged positions of learning at the feet of Christ the Teacher, the disciples did not always grasp his Gospel message. They failed to put their trust in Jesus during the storm at sea (Mk 4:35–41); they were unable to comprehend the miracle of the loaves and fishes (Mk 6:34–44); and, most infamously, prior to Christ's Passion, they abandoned him completely (Mk 14:50).

Yet Christ, the first Christian catechist, showed great patience with the fledgling faith of his students. He saw beyond their human shortcomings and failures. His patient love for them was unending, even unto death. Christ the patient Teacher is a model for teachers and school leaders. We are often frustrated by our students' lack of understanding despite the many hours we spend perfecting our lessons. Sometimes we may be disheartened by the inability of students, their parents, or members of our staff to live the consequences of their faith in their daily lives.

Although their initial years of Christian education were filled with moments of brilliance as well as failure, eventually the disciples became the fearless leaders of the early Church. Christ's example calls us to have the same patience with, and hope for, our students. We must maintain faith that our students will one day grow into a deeper understanding and appreciation of their faith as we recognize God working through them and through us.

PRAYER

Faithful Savior, help us not to become disheartened; keep patience and hope alive in our hearts as we minister to those in our care.

Molly Carlin, MEd, MA
(Queen of Angels Catholic School, Roswell, GA)

The Healing of a Deaf and Mute Man

Mark 7:31–35

Then Jesus returned from the region of Tyre, and went towards the Sea of Galilee. There some people brought to him a deaf man who had an impediment in his speech; and they begged him to lay his hand on him. He took him aside in private, away from the crowd, and put his fingers into his ears, and he spat and touched his tongue. Then looking up to heaven, he sighed and said to him, "Ephphatha," that is, "Be opened!" And immediately his ears were opened, his tongue was released, and he spoke plainly.

When she was nineteen, my mother began to lose her hearing. At age thirty-three, she was declared legally deaf. We frequently prayed for a miraculous healing but, now in her late sixties, her hearing has worsened even with the advances in hearing-aid technologies. In spite of her continued loss, I believe Jesus has answered our prayers and commanded, "Ephphatha!" In doing so, Christ the Teacher has presented a powerful new lesson.

A surface reading of this story might suggest that Jesus did not heal my mother; there has been no physical miracle. But a closer look at Mark's passage suggests that Jesus has healed my mother in a way that is more profound than restored hearing. In Mark's story, Jesus does more than command that the man hear and speak; he cries for him to "Be opened!" That has been Jesus' cry for my mother and our family too.

As Mom's hearing has degenerated, she has gained a whole new sense of listening. She observes people's facial expressions more closely, scrutinizing their lips to distinguish their words and becoming sensitive to their body language. She has learned sign language, taught it to the rest of our family, and helped area parishes begin a signing ministry. She has begun friendships with other people who deal with hearing loss and introduced our family to a whole new community of people. Her world, and ours, has been "opened" because of something most consider a burdensome cross.

With this growth has come a deeper intimacy with God. No longer distracted by sounds and voices, my mother is more introspective and thoughtful. Now she uses the quietness of her physical world to listen more intently to God. This provides her with a spiritual wisdom that is a source of strength and comfort for many people.

In our stress-filled lives, including in our classrooms, we often forget to listen in ways beyond traditional hearing. We jump to conclusions, or flit about from duty to responsibility without acknowledging those around us. We become deaf to what others and God are trying to tell us and become mute when trying to respond. This is the time for us to ask Christ to command, "Ephphatha!"

PRAYER

Father in Heaven, with your "Ephphatha!" quiet us to hear what your Spirit is revealing that we may move into deeper relationship with you.

Stacy Slomski, T.C., MA
(Immaculate Heart of Mary Catholic School, Grand Rapids, MI)

Who Do You Say That I Am?

Matthew 16:13–20

Now when Jesus came into the district of Caesarea Philippi, he asked his disciples, "Who do people say that the Son of Man is?" And they said, "Some say John the Baptist, but others Elijah, and still others Jeremiah or one of the prophets." He said to them, "But who do you say that I am?" Simon Peter answered, "You are the Messiah, the Son of the living God." And Jesus answered him, "Blessed are you, Simon son of Jonah! For flesh and blood has not revealed this to you, but my Father in heaven. And I tell you, you are Peter, and on this rock I will build my church, and the gates of Hades will not prevail against it. I will give you the keys of the kingdom of heaven, and whatever you bind on earth will be bound in heaven, and whatever you loose on earth will be loosed in heaven." Then he sternly ordered the disciples not to tell anyone that he was the Messiah.

Who do you say that I am?" After I began teaching, I remember being asked this question about Jesus on a retreat. I was struck by how much my answer had deepened over the years, moving from a childhood focus solely on Jesus to an adult focus that widened to include me.

I was brought up in a traditional Catholic household with all the images that suggests: weekly Mass, nightly prayers, Catholic schools, Friday fish fries. I came to my first answer to "Who do you say Jesus is?" through such rituals and the way my parents modeled them. Through them, I learned early that Jesus was a compassionate person to worship, to obey, and to love.

As I matured, so did my understanding of the identity of Jesus—perhaps never more so than after I became a teacher. This life made daily demands of me, demands that I increasingly realized I had accepted as a call from Jesus. As a teacher, I truly began to make decisions about how I would spend my life and life's energy. As a teacher, I learned the answer to "Who do you say that I am?" is not only about who Jesus is but who I am. For to confess Jesus as the Christ is also to confess ourselves as his disciples.

In today's reading, Peter answers Jesus' question with courage and passion, "You are the Messiah!" In confessing Jesus as the Christ, Peter is also committing himself as his disciple. So it is with us. To confess ourselves as Jesus' disciples is to recognize that Christ is you and me living and witnessing to the Gospel each day.

It has taken me awhile to get here, but I have come to recognize that my answer to the question "Who do you say that I am?" is not only "You are the Christ" but also "My *life lived* as your disciple." Christ is reflected in the lives devoted to him.

PRAYER

We call you Messiah, Jesus, and so confess ourselves as your disciples. May we be living reflections of all that you are today.

Amy Wyskochil, MEd
(Sacred Heart School, St. Petersburg, FL)

The Transfiguration

Matthew 17:1–9

Six days later, Jesus took with him Peter and James and his brother John and led them up a high mountain, by themselves. And he was transfigured before them, and his face shone like the sun, and his clothes became dazzling white. Suddenly there appeared to them Moses and Elijah, talking with him. Then Peter said to Jesus, "Lord, it is good for us to be here, if you wish, I will make three dwellings here, one for you, one for Moses, and one for Elijah." While he was still speaking, suddenly a bright cloud overshadowed them, and from the cloud a voice said, "This is my Son, the Beloved; with him I am well pleased. Listen to him!" When the disciples heard this, they fell to the ground and were overcome by fear. But Jesus came and touched them, saying, "Get up and do not be afraid." And when they looked up, they saw no one except Jesus himself alone. As they were coming down the mountain, Jesus ordered them, "Tell no one about the vision until after the Son of Man has been raised from the dead."

The Transfiguration is a dramatic moment for Peter, James, and John as they catch a glimpse of Jesus in his true glory. Peter wants to stay on the mountaintop and build shelters there for Jesus, Moses, and Elijah. He wants to remain in that special place for as long as possible, and it's hard to blame him. He means well, but he doesn't quite get it. With a gentle, "Get up and do not be afraid," Jesus reminds his friends that they must come down from the mountain and return to their ministry.

Patience is one characteristic of Christ the Teacher that stands out in this passage. Indeed, this is one of the many episodes—from Peter's asking exactly how many times he must forgive, to his cutting off the ear of the slave in Gethsemane, to his threefold denial of Christ—in which Jesus does not give up on Peter but patiently reminds him of his mission.

We are called to exhibit such patience, especially with those who take longer to understand, and even with ourselves. In the everydayness of our lives and ministry, not every lesson is going to run perfectly, not every student is going to make the grade, not every moment is going to seem as glorious or exciting as the Transfiguration was for the disciples. But this is not a pessimistic outlook. Jesus did not wish his disciples to stay on the mountain and be deluded into thinking that every moment of life shines like the sun. Jesus' vision is a realistic and hopeful one—Christ the Teacher reminds us in the Transfiguration that we need not be afraid to enter fully into the everydayness of ordinary life, because he is patiently with us in all of our experiences, not just those on the mountaintop.

PRAYER

Son of God and Son of Man, thank you for being with us in the everydayness of our lives.

Michael Vanden Boom, MEd
(St. Michael the Archangel High School, Baton Rouge, LA)

The Greatest in the Kingdom of Heaven

Matthew 18:1–3

At that time the disciples came to Jesus and asked, "Who is the greatest in the kingdom of heaven?" He called a child, whom he put among them, and said, "Truly I tell you, unless you change and become like children, you will never enter the kingdom of heaven. Whoever becomes humble like this child is the greatest in the kingdom of heaven. Whoever welcomes one such child in my name welcomes me."

Coaches playing to win at all costs.

Parents fighting in the stands.

Student-athletes displaying poor sportsmanship.

These are unfortunate characteristics of parts of the current youth sport culture. Into the center of it all, Christ the Teacher places an innocent child and asks us to remember what, or rather, who this is all about. Coach-ministers in Christian-sponsored sports leagues have the opportunity to rise above the toxic elements of the popular sports world and commit to honor the grandeur and essentially spiritual nature of children's play in sport. Coaches provide a service to young athletes in lovingly teaching them the physical skills of sport as well as moral virtues that will aid athletes off the field in their Christian lives, forming disciples of the Church and building the kingdom of God.

The character qualities required for excellence in sport are those necessary for becoming a champion in Christian life. Those who coach can learn from Jesus' teaching to become "like little children" as they encourage children's whole growth through their play. When coaches help athletes set and achieve goals, athletes learn fortitude, courage, and persistence. When coaches build positive relationships on sport teams, young people learn justice. Coaches that allow athletes to have ownership over their play empower them by developing prudence, the virtue of wise decision making. Coaches who keep winning in the proper perspective teach athletes temperance. Coaches-as-ministers place the child front and center of all our adult competitions. They educate the children of God in the Christian virtues, thus renewing the whole Church in goodness and reminding each of us that our true destiny as God's children is to one day play with Christ in the kingdom of heaven.

PRAYER

With the openness of children, Father, help us play before you today.

Kristin Komyatte Sheehan, MA
(University of Notre Dame, Notre Dame, IN)

FORGIVENESS

MATTHEW 18:21–22

Then Peter came and said to Jesus, "Lord, if another member of the church sins against me, how often should I forgive? As many as seven times?" Jesus said to him, "Not seven times, but, I tell you, seventy-seven times."

Eighty-seven students.
Four classes to prep.
Thirty-two pages to read.
Forty-eight essays to grade.
Three parents to call.
Fourteen e-mails to reply to.

In my eleven years of teaching, it seems that the exercise of counting has yet to elude me. Despite the fact that I teach English and German, much of my day is filled with numbers. I count the minutes during passing periods; I time students writing journal entries; and about mid-March I begin to count down the days left of school just like my students. I calculate lesson plans, units, assignments, chapters covered, quizzes recorded per quarter, and the number of paragraphs in an essay. So I resonate with this passage in Matthew. Forgive "seventy-seven times"—in other words, forgive without number.

For the most part, my life as a teacher has been blessed, but on occasion a student or two tries my patience and has me gripping my Serenity Prayer card and begging for the grace to forgive. Whether it is an issue of disrespect or someone cheating on a quiz by writing answers on the bottom of a shoe, Jesus' call to forgive without number is a challenge. It is also a constant and often-needed reminder that students deserve forgiveness and a second chance. And, just as important on many days, it is a reminder that teachers do too. A day of last-minute planning, a poorly phrased test question, or a hurried interaction with a struggling student show a teacher's imperfections. Burdened with daily reminders of our limitations, where would we be as teachers without Jesus' seventy-sevenfold healing?

What a blessing that with Christ our Teacher, forgiveness is more than a finite number. He shrugs off Peter's timid suggestion to forgive seven times. His love and forgiveness are infinite. As we receive his forgiveness, we are called to extend it. In Christian education, one thing both teachers and students can count on is forgiveness.

PRAYER

Christ our Teacher, Christ our Savior, may we be ever mindful of the infinite power of forgiveness.

Beth Burau, MEd
(Bishop Lynch High School, Dallas, TX)

A Woman Caught in Adultery

John 8:3–11

The scribes and the Pharisees brought a woman who had been caught in adultery; and making her stand before all of them, they said to Jesus, "Teacher, this woman was caught in the very act of committing adultery. In the law Moses commanded us to stone such women. What do you say?" They said this to test him, to find some charge to bring against him. Jesus bent down and wrote with his finger on the ground. When they kept on questioning him, he straightened up and said, "Let anyone among you who is without sin be the first to throw a stone at her." And again he bent down and wrote on the ground. When they heard it, they went away, one by one, beginning with the elders; and Jesus was left alone with the woman standing before him. Jesus straightened up and said to her, "Woman, where are they? Has no one condemned you?" She said, "No one, sir." And Jesus said, "Neither do I condemn you. Go your way, and from now on do not sin again."

So many of Christ the Teacher's most memorable lessons occur, ironically, when he finds himself being tested by the religious authorities of his time and culture. In such encounters, Jesus is the master of the surprising reversal, typically advanced through an unsuspected question that disrupts the Pharisees' underlying assumptions and the false dilemmas they have designed to entrap him. These religious authorities represent all that good teachers should avoid: impaired faith, limited vision, and disregard for other human beings.

Consider the villainy of the Pharisees' exposure of this woman caught in adultery, not only by the obvious omission of her partner, but by what bears the stench of a horribly premeditated entrapment. It sure looks as though they had schemed in advance and lay in wait for the couple. (How many secrets are there in a small town, after all?) The tension is palpable. *What will the teacher say?*, wonders the gathering crowd, a voyeuristic gang that we, the readers, ought not to distance ourselves from too quickly lest we miss the full impact of the lesson.

And so Jesus takes his time, perhaps because the solution is not easy, but also perhaps because there is a human life at stake here—a daughter of God in Christ's eyes. To answer too quickly is to answer glibly—not a good idea in this volatile scene. And when he does answer, Jesus asks the perfect question of this assembled mob, some no doubt with stones in hand. Through his at once shrewd and compassionate imagination, he finds a response that shifts the terms of their restrictive question. "Which one among you is without sin?"

The woman is saved. And so, potentially, are those who drift away as he writes in the dust. And so are we if we heed Jesus' invitation to compassion borne of the awareness of our own sinfulness and need of God's mercy.

PRAYER

Loving God, grant us the patience, wisdom, and compassion to recognize you in the faces of those we may otherwise rush to condemn.

John Staud, PhD
(University of Notre Dame, Notre Dame, IN)

The Good Shepherd

John 10:11–15

Jesus said, "I am the good shepherd. The good shepherd lays down his life for the sheep. The hired hand, who is not the shepherd and does not own the sheep, sees the wolf coming and leaves the sheep and runs away—and the wolf snatches them and scatters them. The hired hand runs away because a hired hand does not care for the sheep. I am the good shepherd. I know my own and my own know me, just as the Father knows me and I know the Father. And I lay down my life for the sheep."

Jesus tells us a number of things about being the Good Shepherd. That the Good Shepherd knows his sheep and his sheep know him. That the sheep will never follow a stranger—they will run from him because they do not recognize his voice. That, furthermore, the Good Shepherd is willing to lay down his life for the sheep. We in the classroom recognize that it is not only a Good Shepherd whom Jesus describes—it is a great teacher.

We must know our students, and they us, so that they trust us. They learn most willingly from those they trust. We must protect them so they feel safe. They learn most gracefully and freely when they are secure.

And we must, in our own everyday way, lay down our lives for them. They learn most readily—indeed, often enthusiastically—when they can see we care.

Christ the Good Shepherd reminds us that teaching is more than lesson planning, grading, and content matter. Good teachers, like the Good Shepherd, know their students, care about their problems, and commit themselves fully to their success. Good teachers, like the Good Shepherd, are themselves good students. We learn about our pupils by listening to their struggles. We ask questions to learn about who they really are. And we show up. We attend sporting events, concerts, and performances to show them we care about what's important to them. We work tirelessly and endure great turmoil to show them that we are committed to them and their futures. Along the way, something miraculous happens. The Good Shepherd takes form in us and, through us, leads his flock to the pastures where God can most eagerly and satisfyingly be known, loved, and served.

PRAYER

Thank you, Jesus our Good Shepherd, for the opportunity to tend your flock. Give us your courage and commitment as we lead your children to you.

J. J. Gregg, MEd
(Archbishop Carroll High School, Washington, DC)

Jesus and the Children

Mark 10:13–16

People were bringing little children to him in order that he might touch them; and the disciples spoke sternly to them. But when Jesus saw this, he was indignant and said to them, "Let the little children come to me; do not stop them, for it is to such as these that the kingdom of God belongs. Truly I tell you, whoever does not receive the kingdom of God as a little child will never enter it." And he took them up in his arms, laid his hands on them, and blessed them.

In this passage, Jesus tells us that we must be like children to enter heaven. His message runs directly counter to that of this modern age, which constantly tells us to be great, be successful, and be better than others. Little children are not concerned with such things. Yes, my second graders fight at recess over who won the soccer game, and they get upset if some-one cuts in line. But at the end of the day they readily forget about it. Instead, they stand in our prayer circle and offer intentions for their families, each other, and each other's families. This is what Jesus teaches us in this passage: to put aside any notions of competition and judgment and, like little children, rejoice with others in the simple pleasures of life.

On a recent flight home to Florida, the little boy in front of me threw up his arms and shouted, "Yay Tampa!" as he stepped off the airplane. Wow! This child's safe arrival home made him incredibly happy. When we make decisions in our lives that bring us closer to our home (our Father in heaven), can we be childlike enough to experience such joy? Like the child exiting the plane, how can we see the world, and our experience of it, with the beautiful innocence of a child? How can we seek out the good in others and live our lives so we want to shout, "Yay God!" like little children at the end of each day?

PRAYER

You loved children, dear Jesus, and for that we praise you! Help us look at the world with the eyes of a child and notice the beauty that surrounds us.

Marisa Foyle, MEd
(Our Lady of Unity Catholic School, Kansas City, KS)

Jesus' Teaching on Prayer

Luke 11:5–10

When they asked him about prayer, Jesus said to his disciples, "Suppose one of you has a friend, and you go to him at midnight and say to him, 'Friend, lend me three loaves of bread; for a friend of mine has arrived, and I have nothing to set before him.' And he answers from within, 'Do not bother me; the door has already been locked, and my children are with me in bed; I cannot get up and give you anything.' I tell you, even though he will not get up and give him anything because he is his friend, at least because of his persistence he will get up and give him whatever he needs. So I say to you, ask, and it will be given to you; search, and you will find; knock, and the door will be opened for you. For everyone who asks receives, and everyone who searches finds, and for everyone who knocks, the door will be opened."

God, God, God, Jesus, Jesus, Jesus, Lord, Lord, Father, Father, Abba, Abba . . . Hi!"

As teachers we all know what it feels like when one student incessantly taps us on the shoulder while another repeats our name ten times until getting our full attention. Children are persistent in their requests. Even pop culture satirizes this truth using Stewie Griffin in the sitcom, *Family Guy*. Stewie begins, "Mum, mum, mum, mommy, mommy, mommy, mama, mama," as he relentlessly tries to get the attention of his mother simply to say, "Hi."

We too want the Lord to answer us, and Christ reminds us to be like children who are unafraid to ask for the Lord's attention through prayer. "Ask, and you will receive; seek, and you will find; knock, and the door will be opened to you." What do we want that we are not yet asking for? Are we hesitant to seek because we are afraid of what God might help us uncover—or that God might not answer us at all?

Christ the Teacher is constantly reminding his disciples that there is no reason to fear because the Father is *always* welcoming us. Jesus treated the late-night guest with warm hospitality even when the neighbor wanted nothing to do with him. This is the way that the Lord welcomes us—always with generous grace and mercy even when we feel undeserving. God is ready to give not only what we need, but so much more than we could ever begin to imagine.

So let us choose to accept grace daily. Let us choose to seek with persistence and intentionality. Let us always remember that God wants nothing more than to welcome us, even in the middle of the night, and to answer every single time we call his name.

PRAYER

God of dark and light, make our hearts new and bold to call your name in the darkness of the night.

Kate Linden, MEd
(Creighton University, Omaha, NE)

Do Not Worry

Luke 12:22–24, 29–34

Jesus said to his disciples, "Do not worry about your life, what you will eat, or about your body, what you will wear. For life is more than food, and the body more than clothing. Consider the ravens: they neither sow nor reap, they have neither storehouse nor barn, and yet God feeds them. Of how much more value are you than the birds! Do not keep striving for what you are to eat and what you are to drink, and do not keep worrying. For the nations of the world strive after all these things, and your Father knows that you need them. Instead, strive for his kingdom, and these things will be given to you as well. Do not be afraid, little flock, for it is your Father's good pleasure to give you the kingdom. Sell your possessions, and give alms. Make purses for yourselves that do not wear out, an unfailing treasure in heaven, where no thief comes near and no moth destroys. For where your treasure is, there your heart will be also."

It seems written in our nature to worry about that which is beyond our control, to consciously or unconsciously doubt that we will be provided for, to falter in the face of setbacks, wondering where God is in the midst of the struggle. We profess in our word and vocation trust in the example and direction of Christ the Teacher; yet, just as willingly as we give him our troubles we quickly take them back in a flurry of doubts.

As educators of the whole person, we experience that carousel of questions and worries in a raw and sometimes relentless way. Will my students get what they need to flourish in this life and the next? Can I provide the love and guidance they deserve? Are my skills and intentions enough? Do I have the strength of mind and heart to emulate the one true Teacher? But as humans and passionate individuals committed to the mission of Christ the Teacher, we must calibrate our real and restless questions in accordance with Jesus' clear and direct words: do not worry about your life. Jesus urges us to seek single-heartedly his kingdom and these other things will be given to us. Where our treasure is, there will be our heart.

Let us breathe deeply this mantra—*do not worry about your life*—and live out the message to seek first the kingdom, in and through all people, places, and struggles. Let us know always that Christ the Teacher watches over us, provides for us, gently guiding us through every worry, big and small. Christ will provide the energy and strength we require, not for useless worry about ourselves, but for his children—our treasure—and the renewal of the kingdom through them.

PRAYER

Free our minds and hearts from worry, we pray, and help us wholeheartedly seek you today.

Kathleen Davidson, MEd
(Resurrection Catholic School, Pascagoula, MS)

Jesus Heals the Woman Crippled by a Spirit

Luke 13:10–13

Now Jesus was teaching in one of the synagogues on the Sabbath. Just then there appeared a woman with a spirit that had crippled her for eighteen years. She was bent over and was quite unable to stand up straight. Jesus called her over and said, "Woman, you are set free from your ailment." When he laid his hands on her, immediately she stood up straight and began praising God.

This reading highlights Christ's healing of a woman crippled for two decades. The passage does not immediately depict Christ as Teacher, although his exchange with the woman occurs amid his more formal teaching to his disciples, as well as to those in the synagogue on the Sabbath. The story beautifully expresses Christ's ability to truly see others and enter into their suffering. But how does it bear relevance in the life and ministry of a teacher?

Luke's sandwiching of Christ's healing action between the parables of the fig tree and mustard seed highlights Christ's authenticity as a teacher. Jesus not only *preached* the need for societal transformation ("For three years now I have come looking for fruit on this fig tree, and still I find none. [So] cut it down!" [Lk 13:7]) and for radical inclusivity to bring about God's kingdom ("It is like a mustard seed that someone took and sowed in the garden; it grew and became a tree, and the birds of the air made nests in its branches" [Lk 13:19]), at every opportunity, he *practiced* both a justice and an empathy mirroring God's reign.

In first-century Jerusalem, Jesus' respectful attention to not only a woman but a woman experiencing noticeable injury was tremendously countercultural. Women, and all people not in good physical and/or mental health, were shunned. As theologian Elizabeth Johnson notes in her book *Consider Jesus*, "Those on the periphery of established structures are counted first in the reign of God . . . to break the old pattern of (societal) discrimination and set up a new pattern of relating." Jesus not only addresses the woman—he treats her with genuine dignity.

Students of all ages are perceptive; students watch their parents and teachers, intuitively discerning how their words align with their actions. And we parents and teachers see reflected in our children and students our own expressions, behaviors, and teaching. It is beautiful to realize that this imitation can also happen to us when we—as God's children and Jesus' students—lovingly absorb the words and actions of

Christ. In restoring not only the physical health but the dignity of the woman in this story, Jesus invited every onlooker to experience, and to imitate, the transforming love and healing of God's kingdom.

Dante called Luke "the scribe of Christ's gentleness"—even as he wrote about Jesus' radically controversial preaching and actions. In this healing story, Luke offers us this enlightening paradox of Jesus. The alignment of Christ's challenging words with his gentle actions moves his disciples to conversion and imitation. Authentic teachers not only inform but transform their students and their communities. Authentic teachers call others to follow a powerful, yet gentle, Christ the Teacher.

PRAYER

We long to be authentic, Jesus, as you were authentic. May both our words and our actions be of your making.

Andrea Ray Alessio, MEd, MA, MPA
(Holy Names Academy, Seattle, WA)

Jesus at a Pharisee's House

Luke 14:1–6

On one occasion when Jesus was going to the house of a leader of the Pharisees to eat a meal on the Sabbath, they were watching him closely. Just then, in front of him, there was a man who had dropsy. And Jesus asked the lawyers and Pharisees, "Is it lawful to cure people on the Sabbath, or not?" But they were silent. So Jesus took him and healed him, and sent him away. Then he said to them, "If one of you has a child or an ox that has fallen into a well, will you not immediately pull it out on a Sabbath day?" And they could not reply to this.

Christ the Teacher never asks a question to which he does not know the answer. Rather, he asks a question so that those who answer might learn something about him. In one place, for instance, he asks, "Who do you say that I am?" (Mt 16:15) and in another, "What do you want me to do for you?" (Mk 10:51). As disciples, we can learn much from the responses given. To the first question, Peter responds, "You are the Messiah, the Son of the living God" (Mt 16:16), and to the second question, the blind man replies, "My teacher, let me see again" (Mk 10:51).

We find in this passage, though, that in response to Jesus' question, "Is it lawful to cure people on the Sabbath, or not?" Jesus' listeners "were silent." Did our Lord give adequate wait time? His pedagogically effective question certainly asked for a high level of self-reflection on the part of his hearers. As a teacher, it is easy to become uncomfortable with the silence while waiting for a response. The strong temptation is to answer our own questions and keep moving.

Our Lord, however, does not do that. Instead, again providing first-class pedagogy, he provides a real-life demonstration, reframing the question to make it more concrete. "If one of you has a child or an ox that has fallen into a well, will you not immediately pull it out on a Sabbath day?" Still, and surely frustratingly, "they could not reply to this." Christ the Teacher allows the question to hang suspended in their souls. The answer will not come today, but perhaps this seed he has sown will sprout some future day. He seems willing to wait. He is a master teacher.

Surely in this passage there is a pedagogical technique about wait time we can learn as teachers, but what about as his children? What about those times when we ask questions of our Lord that seem to go unanswered? Do we practice adequate wait time? Or do we grow uncomfortable with the silence and seek to answer the questions ourselves? When these times come, may Christ the Teacher give us the grace to "be patient, therefore, beloved, until the coming of the Lord . . . [for he is] compassionate and merciful" (Jas 5:7, 11). May Christ the Teacher remind us to be steadfast, granting us the eagerness and strength to wait, as he did, for the seeds of God's answers to sprout within us.

PRAYER

Lord Jesus, when questions overwhelm us, grant us the patience to wait for your response, trusting in your compassion and mercy.

Karl Hendrickson, MEd
(Saint Agnes School, Saint Paul, MN)

The Parable of the Lost Sheep

Matthew 18:10–14

Jesus said to his disciples, "Take care that you do not despise one of these little ones; for I tell you, in heaven their angels continually see the face of my Father in heaven. What do you think? If a shepherd has a hundred sheep, and one of them has gone astray, does he not leave the ninety-nine on the mountains and go in search of the one that went astray? And if he finds it, truly I tell you, he rejoices over it more than over the ninety-nine that never went astray. So it is not the will of your Father in heaven that one of these little ones should be lost."

As every schoolteacher and administrator knows, occasionally it's necessary to expel a student. And sometimes we're relieved to do so. I have at times found myself among those calling for a student to be shown the door. But with each year of teaching, I find myself drawn more to the students who seem on the verge of dismissal. The Christ of this passage—who with great inconvenience goes looking for his one lost sheep—is the kind of teacher I strive to be because he is a teacher who sees the inherent worth in every child.

As teachers, we are only human. Sometimes we can let our emotions get the better of us, leading us to react negatively or dismissively to a disruptive child. At these times, it is often easier to reason that the child must not be fit for our school (or at least for our classroom or line of vision that day) than it is to attempt to understand the underlying reasons for the child's behavior. It is often easier to see those who are succeeding and take credit for teaching them than it is to see those who are failing and take some responsibility.

Yet, in Christ's eyes there are no hopeless causes, no unteachable students, just lost children looking for a teacher who will have the patience and love to pick them up when they fall, a teacher who will recognize, celebrate, and validate their worth as students and individuals. Jesus does not merely tolerate such children; he seeks them out and, if this gospel is to be believed, takes a particular joy in them. Let us pray that God will grace us with the patience, perseverance, and empathy we need to seek out and rejoice in the gifts of each of our students.

PRAYER

Make us ever watchful, faithful Savior, so that we may extend a hand to those who stray.

Colleen Gannon, MEd
(Washington Jesuit Academy, Washington, DC)

When the Lost Sheep Is Found

Luke 15:1–7

Now all the tax-collectors and sinners were coming near to listen to Jesus. And the Pharisees and the scribes were grumbling and saying, "This fellow welcomes sinners and eats with them." So he told them this parable: "Which one of you, having a hundred sheep and losing one of them, does not leave the ninety-nine in the wilderness and go after the one that is lost until he finds it? When he has found it, he lays it on his shoulders and rejoices. And when he comes home, he calls together his friends and neighbors, saying to them, 'Rejoice with me, for I have found my sheep that was lost.' Just so, I tell you, there will be more joy in heaven over one sinner who repents than over ninety-nine righteous people who need no repentance."

Between people, forgiveness is often bestowed reluctantly, begrudgingly. Perhaps we secretly believe God behaves this way too. Admitting sins to God is like showing a scar, the Sacrament of Reconciliation like an after-school accounting with your principal, an act of penance like detention. But Christ revealed the joy with which God forgives. "There will be more joy in heaven over one sinner who repents than over ninety-nine righteous people who have no need of repentance."

I never understood this teaching until I had to forgive Eric. Eric was stocky and silly and sincere. His well-placed antics kept the seventh grade, and me, lighthearted. In math class, he would answer the few questions he knew in earnest. Unfortunately this couldn't keep him from nearly failing. So, one day, Eric cheated on his math test.

The next day, I told the class I suspected some people had cheated on the test and that it would be better for them if they came forward before I came to them. After class, when the other students had gone, Eric lingered by my desk. I pretended I didn't know what he would say. "What's up?" I asked. He stuck out his chin and took one step backward. "I," he said, his eyes welling up with tears, "cheated."

At that moment, I was surprised to discover there was nothing but joy for Eric in my heart. How could I express to him how proud I was, how little the cheating mattered now, how much I had watched him grow in that one moment by wrestling with his pride and fear? I finally understood heaven's joy.

I go to the Lord with my sins much more easily now.

PRAYER

Where would we be, dear Jesus, without your willingness to welcome sinners? Thank you for the gift of forgiveness!

Barbara Jane Sloan, MEd
(Holy Spirit Preparatory School, Atlanta, GA)

Ten Healed of Leprosy

Luke 17:11–19

As Jesus entered a village on his way to Jerusalem, ten lepers approached him. Keeping their distance, they called out, saying, "Jesus, Master, have mercy on us!" When he saw them, he said to them, "Go and show yourselves to the priests." And as they went, they were made clean. Then one of them, when he saw that he was healed, turned back, praising God with a loud voice. He prostrated himself at Jesus' feet and thanked him. And he was a Samaritan. Then Jesus asked, "Were not ten made clean? But the other nine, where are they?" Then he said to him, "Your faith has made you well."

Some years ago, a mentor of mine reminded me incessantly that I should see everything with an *attitude of gratitude*. Initially, I got a kick out of it, but repeated thousands of times in an unending chorus, the phrase got under my skin. It clung to me in the classroom. Did your car break down on the way to school? *Attitude of gratitude.* Lost your stack of graded papers? *Attitude of gratitude.* Angry parent call you at home as you sit down to dinner? *Attitude of gratitude.*

Nothing was exempt. No matter how banal or frustrating the reality, this stubborn guide of mine insisted that I say thank you for it all—for the neighbor who helped me with my broken-down car, for the chance to admit to my students that I lose things too, for the many parents who are eager to support me. The message, of course, is simple awareness that God is with us in all things.

This parable in the Gospel of Luke reminds us of that simple truth: we make things holy by giving thanks for them. The leper cries out to Christ for compassion and healing. And then he does something truly astonishing as the others run ahead in haste: he sees that he has been healed and takes the time to give thanks.

We are all healed by Christ too, or perhaps more accurately, we are all being healed; our lives are in constant contact with the living God. Like the leper in the story, we are called to realize that we are being healed and to lift our voices to God in thanks and praise, and not just when life gives us moments to celebrate. In every hour, even when we've been turned away, disappointed, or lulled into the myth of the mundane, we should give thanks.

Of course, it is unimaginably hard to do this, to give thanks that the most commonplace, everyday occurrences are "charged with the grandeur of God." To do it, we have to look at who we are and who and what God has put in front of us. Like the leper, we have to see that we, our students, and our colleagues are surrounded by God's healing love in every activity, in every common bit of creation. We are utterly immersed in God's presence. It is here. It is now. "Rise and go. Your faith has made you well."

PRAYER

Lord, like the leper who returned with praise on his lips, make us aware of our healing today, and teach us to give thanks.

Andrew Hoyt
(Cristo Rey Jesuit College Preparatory School of Houston,Houston, TX)

Jesus' Rejection in Nazareth

Matthew 13:54–58

Jesus came to his hometown and taught the people in their synagogue. They were astonished and said, "Where did this man get such wisdom and mighty deeds. Is he not the carpenter's son? Is not his mother named Mary and his brothers James, Joseph, Simon, and Judas? Are not his sisters all with us? Where did this man get all this?" And they took offense at him. But Jesus said to them, "A prophet is not without honor except in his native place and in his own house." And he did not work many mighty deeds there because of their lack of faith.

Teaching is a humbling experience. In my first year as a middle school social studies and religion teacher, students fed on my doubts, fears, and failures. Some of them even took offense to what I taught—a problem, one would think, that math teachers never seem to have!

As a teacher, it's easy to doubt yourself. It's easy to feel like you're not good enough. You put yourself on the line all the time and risk failure and sometimes even humiliation. You get rejected. Not every student believes or even cares about what you say. Positive feedback is often lacking. At times like these, we are Jesus in his hometown of Nazareth.

Imagine yourself in Jesus' shoes. You've just spent months astonishing people with your teaching. You have amassed thousands of followers who cling to your every word. Then you make a triumphant return home to share this message with the people who you know best, only to be rejected as an imposter. These people think they know who you are. You are a carpenter, not a teacher.

It is natural to feel like you're an imposter—that you don't really know what you're talking about. It is easy to tell yourself you're not good enough. But Jesus didn't think that way. He was determined. He continued teaching and performing miracles in his Father's name despite the rejection.

A constant theme in both the Old and New Testaments is dependence on God. The source of Jesus' identity and work was in God the Father, not in the apparent success and failure, praise and rejection, of his daily life. When we doubt ourselves, let us turn to God, the true source of our identity. God will be the source of everything we need in our ministry, including our fortitude and self-assurance in the face of ingratitude or rejection.

PRAYER

Humble Savior, convict us of our brokenness so that we depend on you. Deliver us from evil and lead us by the light of your truth.

Jared Dees, MEd
(Pope John Paul II High School, Hendersonville, TN)

For God All Things Are Possible

Matthew 19:24–26

Then Jesus said to his disciples, "Truly I tell you, it will be hard for a rich person to enter the kingdom of heaven. Again I tell you, it is easier for a camel to go through the eye of a needle than for someone who is rich to enter the kingdom of God." When the disciples heard this, they were greatly astounded and said, "Then who can be saved?" But Jesus looked at them and said, "For mortals it is impossible, but for God all things are possible."

In this day and age, teachers are given the daunting task of being everything to every child. We are to be the disciplinarians who teach children about what is right and just, even though they live in a world that is often prejudiced and cruel. We are to teach children how to make good choices, although they are surrounded by temptations. We are to nurse them in body and spirit, although they often do not have enough food to eat or adequate attention given to them. We are to help them have pride in themselves and in their work, when all they feel is despair at their incompetence. We are to teach them about math, science, reading, and social studies, when all that seems relevant is the art of survival. We are told that it is our job to do all this, despite budget cuts, rising class sizes, increasing expectations from both parents and administrators, and growing student needs. We are to do this with patience, kindness, thoughtfulness, and an ever-ready smile.

Improbable, yes. Impossible, no. When Jesus said, "For mortals it is impossible, but for God all things are possible," he was talking about salvation, but he surely must have also been thinking of teachers! I believe this because all over the world, despite all the odds, teachers continue to shape children's lives with their hope and enthusiasm. I believe this because, like other dedicated teachers, I trust that, when nurtured, students will not only survive—they will thrive. I believe this because I have witnessed students who, facing even the most difficult of circumstances, have graduated to become successful, Christian members of society. Teaching has its crosses, but it has its amazing blessings too. Teach long enough, and the truth of Christ's saying here becomes incarnate before our eyes, through our students: for God, all things certainly are possible!

PRAYER

Thank you, Christ Jesus, that through you we have the daily blessing of hope.

Ellen Riley, MEd
(St. Michael the Archangel, Leawood, KS)

The Rich Young Man

Mark 10:17–22

As Jesus was setting out on a journey, a man ran up and knelt before him, and asked him, "Good Teacher, what must I do to inherit eternal life?" Jesus said to him, "Why do you call me good? No one is good but God alone. You know the commandments: you shall not murder; you shall not commit adultery; you shall not steal; you shall not bear false witness; you shall not defraud; honor your father and mother." He said to him, "Teacher, I have kept all these since my youth." Jesus, looking at him, loved him and said, "You lack one thing; go, sell what you own, and give the money to the poor, and you will have treasure in heaven; then come, follow me." When he heard this, he was shocked and went away grieving, for he had many possessions.

After assigning independent work in my fourth-grade classroom, it is usually only a matter of minutes before the fastest workers of the bunch start to eagerly approach me to ask that dreaded question: "Now what?" After running through the list of "Did you double-check your work?" and "Are you sure you did both sides?" and "Did you do it in cursive?" only to be met with responses of "Yes," "Yes," and "Of course," I manage to stall long enough to dream up a challenge for these students who seem to beg for more.

At the same time, I am met with students who are always just off the mark. Some work is missing. Something is wrong. Some attitude or behavior needs correction. Her desk is messy. He forgot his PE clothes (again). Those two are still talking in the back row.

In this reading, the interaction of Christ the Teacher with his disciple (who seems at once to embody the best and worst in my students) challenges me to examine my own interactions with students on both ends of the spectrum. The young man approaches Christ seeking eternal life, and Christ reminds his pupil of the usual commandments. When the young man responds with the same, "Yes," "Yes," and "Of course," Christ, who intimately knows the student's heart and all his potential, poses the most difficult challenge to him: to sell everything and come follow him. Though the bar is high and the disciple not quite up to the task, it is not with harsh words or a condescending voice that Jesus points out his shortcoming. In fact, Mark says succinctly and beautifully, "Jesus, looking at him, loved him."

I ask myself: Do my interactions with students reflect Christ's love as revealed in its broad range in this passage? When I challenge students, is it with a zealous hope in their potential? When I correct students, is it with the loving eyes of Christ the Teacher? Are my interactions with coworkers, parents, family members, or friends viewed through the same eyes of love? May Christ the Teacher both look upon us and endow us with eyes of love today.

PRAYER

Christ, our generous Lord, thank you for your deep love for us. By your Spirit make us models of that love to whomever crosses our path.

Elizabeth Stewart, MEd
(St. Monica Catholic School, Dallas, TX)

The Unreachable Student

Luke 18:18–23

A certain ruler asked Jesus, "Good Teacher, what must I do to inherit eternal life?" Jesus said to him, "Why do you call me good? No one is good but God alone. You know the commandments: you shall not commit adultery; you shall not murder; you shall not steal; you shall not bear false witness; honor your father and mother." He replied, "I have kept all these since my youth." When Jesus heard this, he said to him, "There is still one thing lacking. Sell all that you own and distribute the money to the poor, and you will have treasure in heaven; then come, follow me." But when he heard this, he became sad, for he was very rich.

The clock would tick past nine, ten, midnight, and sometimes past two in the morning. I would be at my desk in my house working on lessons, going over assessments, or rereading textbooks. These long nights would be the result of a few students who weren't grasping what I was trying to teach them. I felt they were failing, and I felt I was failing as a teacher. I thought I—and they—could become perfect if I spent one more hour working on the next lesson.

In today's story from Luke's gospel, we see Jesus, the Good Teacher, assessing the man who wants eternal life, who seeks perfection. The man obviously paid attention to his past teachers (he knows all the right answers), but sometimes even the best students do not grasp the breadth and depth of what you are trying to teach them. Jesus tries again to teach the man how to gain eternal life. "Sell what you have and give to the poor." Still, the man does not understand.

Like all of us who have spent late nights revising failed lesson plans, Jesus must have been disappointed. Somehow, it is consoling to think he shares this experience with us. Though disappointed, and though perhaps he never reaches this disciple, he perseveres in his teaching ministry. And, as the same story in Mark's gospel makes clear, Jesus extends his limitless love. "Jesus, looking at him, loved him."

Jesus gives everything in order to teach his disciples. He is the model teacher, yet not every one of his students masters the lesson. We know his frustration. Can we also know his perseverance and limitless love? As teachers, we sometimes work late nights and early mornings trying to perfect our lesson plans. Yet, we realize that if Jesus did not reach every disciple, then neither will we. So we can take comfort in this: through our persistence and faithfulness to our teaching ministry, even as we attempt and perhaps fail to reach the unreachable student, we grow more like the Good Teacher.

PRAYER

Good and gracious Teacher, give us the perseverance to do your will, even when we think we are failing.

Anthony Barber, MEd
(Bishop Ward High School, Kansas City, KS)

The Request of James and John

Mark 10:35–39, 42–45

The disciples James and John came to Jesus and said, "Teacher, we want you to do for us whatever we ask of you." He said to them, "What is it you want me to do for you?" And they said, "Grant us to sit, one at your right hand and one at your left, in your glory." But Jesus said to them, "You do not know what you are asking. Are you able to drink the cup that I drink, or be baptized with the baptism that I am baptized with?" They replied, "We are." Then Jesus said to them, "You know that among the Gentiles those whom they recognize as their rulers lord it over them, and their great ones are tyrants over them. But it is not so among you. Whoever wishes to become great among you must be your servant, and whoever wishes to be first among you must be slave of all. For the Son of Man came not to be served but to serve, and to give his life a ransom for many."

When I think of Christ the Teacher, I usually concentrate on his perfection as a teacher. Since he is God, he must have taught his disciples in the best possible way. It hadn't occurred to me until I started teaching that Christ's disciples listened to him about as well as a bunch of middle school students sometimes do, and perhaps worse.

In this gospel passage, which follows directly after Jesus' third prediction of his Passion, two of his closest apostles still don't have a clue that there is going to be a Passion. They are caught up in the glory and excitement of a Christ who will rule Israel and appoint them as chief assistants. They have not listened to anything that he has been saying. It reminds me of my classroom. After I have explained directions for a project two times and then asked a student to re-explain the directions to the entire class, inevitably another student will ask, "So, what are we supposed to do?"

It is the same for Jesus here. Except in his case, it's not a simple project that his students will fail if they don't listen; it's the beginning of the Church. Despite the pressure, Jesus doesn't become frustrated or angry with his apostles. He explains for what must have felt like the hundredth time that those who wish to be first must be last and the servants of all. We know that eventually the apostles get it because Christ's death on the cross (though even that took the Resurrection appearances and Pentecost). We know that eventually we ourselves have gotten it. And we trust that, through our patient example, our students will get it too.

PRAYER

Lord, we praise you for your love for and patience with us. Help us to await eagerly the revelation of your glory.

Theresa Klinkhammer, MEd
(St. Pius X, Mobile, AL)

The Parable of the Workers in the Vineyard

Matthew 20:1–6, 8–11, 13, 15–16

Jesus told his disciples this story: "The kingdom of heaven is like a landowner who went out early in the morning to hire laborers for his vineyard. After agreeing with them on the usual daily wage, he sent them into his vineyard. When he went out about nine o'clock, he saw others standing idle in the market-place; and he said to them, 'You also go into the vineyard, and I will pay you whatever is right.' So they went. When he went out again about noon, three o'clock, and five o'clock, he did the same. When evening came, the owner of the vineyard said to his manager, 'Call the laborers and give them their pay, beginning with the last and then going to the first.' When those hired about five o'clock came, each of them received the usual daily wage. When the first came, they thought they would receive more; but each of them also received the usual daily wage. And they grumbled against the landowner. But he replied to one of them, 'Friend, am I not allowed to do what I choose with what belongs to me? Or are you envious because I am generous?' So the last will be first, and the first will be last."

In this parable, Christ the Teacher raises questions about the standard of justice in the kingdom of God and provides an important reminder to those of us who rightfully seek success in the classroom. Evidently, entry into the kingdom of God is not a question of personal merit. Justification and sanctification are gifts. So how do we get into the kingdom if it is not something that we can earn? We simply consent to God's invitation.

Here grace is symbolized by the mysterious need of the landowner for more workers. Grace, in this sense, is God's need to respond to our need. God's response is directed to the people standing in the marketplace, idle and wasting their time. Their *behavior* does not merit anything, but their *need* is great. It is their need that Jesus is responding to. Hence, his response subverts our idea of how to win God's favor. We do not win it by teaching better, by having perfect lesson plans, by reaching every student. God's mercy is evoked in direct proportion to our need—to our lack of inner and outer resources.

The bottom line is that the fallen human condition is where the kingdom is most active. It is not based on human effort or standards of justice and equity, but on the infinite mercy of God. The kingdom is a sheer gift of God's boundless compassion. We are justified not by our greatness as teachers but by God's divine greatness.

This parable announces that human standards of judgment have no place in the kingdom. A new standard is present, which is God's infinite need to show us mercy. May Christ our Teacher open our hearts and minds to this great teaching.

PRAYER

Open us, God, to your presence in our lives. Help us to know that everything is a gift, most especially your kingdom.

Fr. Joe Corpora, C.S.C.
(University of Notre Dame, Notre Dame, IN)

The Mother of James and John

Matthew 20:20–22, 24–28

Then the mother of James and John, the sons of Zebedee, came to Jesus with her sons, and kneeling before him, she asked a favor of him. And he said to her, "What do you want?" She said to him, "Declare that these two sons of mine will sit, one at your right hand and one at your left, in your kingdom." But Jesus answered, "You do not know what you are asking. Are you able to drink the cup that I am about to drink?" They said, "We are." When the ten heard it, they were angry with the two brothers. But Jesus called them to him and said, "You know that the rulers of the Gentiles lord it over them, and their great ones are tyrants over them. It will not be so among you; but whoever wishes to be great among you must be your servant, and whoever wishes to be first among you must be your slave; just as the Son of Man came not to be served but to serve, and to give his life a ransom for many."

Any teacher who has held parent-teacher conferences has met the mother of the sons of Zebedee.

It is understandable that parents are concerned about their children's futures. Yet, in her question we see the seeds of a larger cultural problem. As Dietrich Bonhoeffer put it in his book *Life Together*, "It is the struggle for natural man for self-justification. He finds it only in comparing himself with others, in condemning and judging others." By wishing her children to sit at Christ's right and left hands, this mother is implicitly asking that others not have that privilege. And the ten are resentful that their mothers didn't think of it first!

But then Christ's instructive revelation comes. God does not look for those who can jump the highest or who have the biggest audience. He is not interested in who gets the gold star or first place. He doesn't even care who the valedictorian is. To be great in God's eyes, we must become servants. This flies directly in the face of what we learn from American culture and generally in American schools. In a society where service programs are touted for what we ourselves can get out of them, not getting credit for our good deeds can seem intolerable.

Every teacher has a daily opportunity to serve the least of our brothers and sisters—for every student by definition is in need. We serve Christ by honoring the students who struggle academically, athletically, and socially. Are teachers aptly rewarded for this most noble service they provide? When we are not, Christ the Teacher invites us not to become discouraged or embittered, but to stay focused on what truly brings life—our service to those most in need.

PRAYER

Dear Lord, please help us in our moments of pride to remember that our service is not for ourselves but for your glory.

Jennifer Borek, PhD
(University of Notre Dame, Notre Dame, IN)

The First Shall Be Last

Luke 22:24–27

A dispute also arose among the disciples as to which one of them was to be regarded as the greatest. But Jesus said to them, "The kings of the Gentiles lord it over them; and those in authority over them are called benefactors. But not so with you; rather the greatest among you must become like the youngest, and the leader like one who serves. For who is greater, the one who is at the table or the one who serves? Is it not the one at the table? But I am among you as one who serves."

From the first lesson I taught, I realized teaching was the avenue I was called to follow in order to satiate the hunger to serve. I felt something ignite inside me that first day of class. I felt the Spirit move me as I instructed a group of high school students in the "classroom" of a chalk-lined softball field. I felt energy when I knelt in the dirt and explained the fundamentals of fielding a ground ball. I felt a burning sensation in my chest as I observed the imaginary light bulb illuminate when I taught an athlete how to hit. This inspiration within me became a way to connect with the person of Jesus.

I believe Christ the Teacher felt that burning energy every time he served his people. Christ was so passionate about serving us that he put himself last so that we may be first. He knew the best way for *us* to learn was not so much to tell us how to live but to show us. As he served us, he taught us. Christ was the consummate Servant Teacher. And what he taught us is that our lives too will be most vibrant, charged, and fulfilling when we serve as he served.

In our classrooms, on our playing fields, in our homes and communities, we follow this Christ, the Servant Teacher. To serve means to help, to render assistance, and to give. Everyone in need who approaches us becomes an invitation from Christ to be his hands and feet. To be a disciple of Christ is to enroll in a school that educates in the way of love. Christ assists us in our development as humble human beings. Most importantly, Christ gives his life so that we may live.

Today may we follow his lead and be teachers, not tellers. May Christ ignite our energy and guide us to wholeheartedly serve those who need him most. And may he help us share our gifts so that our students recognize Christ as their Teacher.

PRAYER

You gave us, dear Jesus, the desire to serve. By your Spirit, keep the passion alive in us each day.

Christy Connoyer, MAT
(Saint Louis University, St. Louis, MO)

Jesus Clears the Temple

John 2:13–17

The Passover of the Jews was near, and Jesus went up to Jerusalem. In the temple he found people selling cattle, sheep, and doves, and the money-changers seated at their tables. Making a whip of cords, he drove all of them out of the temple, both the sheep and the cattle. He also poured out the coins of the money-changers and overturned their tables. He told those who were selling the doves, "Take these things out of here! Stop making my Father's house a marketplace!" His disciples remembered that it was written, "Zeal for your house will consume me."

When looking at Christ as a teacher, we often encounter an impossibly steady role model. He is always kind, consistently humble, and patiently persistent. Jesus abandoned himself totally to love even those who proved through sin or stigma to be difficult to embrace. These are admirable qualities that every teacher strives to attain. Yet there are days when the most even-tempered instructor runs short of second chances. Patience flees. Anger and frustration emerge. And though we might well be justified, we feel guilty for not being more Christ-like in our demeanor.

We forget, though, that even the Messiah was an emotional man.

Jesus' entrance into the temple shows an often-overlooked side of the Savior, one of holy, purposeful frustration. The temple area had been transformed into a marketplace; the sacredness of the institution had been defiled. The appropriate response was not one of benign resignation or patient equilibrium, but one of God-centered pain and anger. Consumed by zeal, Jesus was firm in his correction and returned the temple to a place of worship.

How effective would we be as teachers if we permitted ourselves the same zeal for our classroom that Christ had for his Father's house? He saw the same untapped potential in the temple—an encounter with God—that we see in our schools, our classrooms, and our students. He also illustrated that while love is most often tender, it cannot fear to be bold. Perhaps some holy anger could on occasion produce a similarly cathartic experience for our students and transform some of the more listless parts of our ministry, from unjust educational structures to deficient resources, into opportunities for a zealous communion with the Creator.

PRAYER

Father God, send forth your Spirit and consume our hearts with zeal so that we may respond to each hour of this day with the fervor of Christ.

Cory Irwin, MEd
(Richmond High School, Richmond, IN)

Jesus at the Temple

Matthew 21:15–17

But when the chief priests and the scribes saw the amazing things that he did, and heard the children crying out in the temple, "Hosanna to the Son of David," they became angry and said to him, "Do you hear what these are saying?" Jesus said to them, "Yes; have you never read, 'Out of the mouths of infants and nursing babies you have prepared praise for yourself'?" He left them, went out of the city to Bethany, and spent the night there.

Who among us are the most blessed? Perhaps teachers know more readily than most: the children, of course! They are blessed with the gifts of innocence, simplicity, and honest joy. These gifts come wrapped in God's revelations that can often be lost on us, the wise and learned.

How do I know? Just think about the differences between children and adults. Tell a child something astonishing and wonderful and she accepts it at face value. Tell an adult the same thing and she becomes skeptical and unbelieving. Share a happy secret with a child and he giggles with delight. Tell an adult and he becomes guarded and wary. Ask a child to help you and she is more than willing to please you. Ask an adult and chances are he will have a multitude of reasons why he cannot. Is it any wonder, then, that God chose to reveal himself and his splendor so lavishly to children?

I am blessed to be a teacher. I experience my students' unconditional acceptance on a daily basis. I am in awe of their joyful exuberance. They are ready and open to know God with enthusiasm and delight. Failures and disappointments have not yet eaten away at the beauty of life. They are still in love with the Father. Jesus teaches, "Out of the mouths of [children] you have prepared praise for yourself." In our daily service, may Christ give us eyes that do not overlook these preachers of his Word and ears to hear their songs of praise.

PRAYER

Guide those of us you have entrusted with your precious children, dear Father, so that when we look at them, we see and hear you.

Mary Johnson, MEd
(St. Michael Academy, San Diego, CA)

Zacchaeus the Tax Collector

Luke 19:1–6

Jesus entered Jericho and was passing through it. A man was there named Zacchaeus; he was a chief tax-collector and was rich. He was trying to see who Jesus was, but on account of the crowd he could not, because he was short in stature. So he ran ahead and climbed a sycamore tree to see him, because he was going to pass that way. When Jesus came to the place, he looked up and said to him, "Zacchaeus, hurry and come down; for I must stay at your house today." So he hurried down and was happy to welcome him.

Zacchaeus, known to many as the "wee little man," wanted to see Jesus, but he could not for he was "short in stature." He was not only physically short, but he was short sighted and without much meaning in his life. As a wealthy tax collector who was hated for bilking people out of their hard-earned wages, he experienced a worse kind of poverty than those without money: he was cut off from his community, living an invisible life.

Though he wanted to see Jesus, it was Jesus who saw him. Zacchaeus was visible to Jesus and, as always, Christ saw him for who he was, just as he sees us for who we are.

Where I work, at a homeless shelter, I get calls all the time from folks who talk about the visible problem of homelessness we have in our community. People say that there are more and more homeless men and women just hanging out for all the public to see. This, they say, is a problem that we want to see less of.

Tonight I ran into a guest I haven't seen in a while. He had been away from our facility and has now returned with passion and focus on his future. I immediately said how great it was to see him. He looked at me and said, "It's great to be seen."

These five words—it's great to be seen—are powerful enough to change lives. I can imagine Zacchaeus saying these words to Jesus when he climbed down from his tree.

In the book *The Missing Class*, authors Katherine Newman and Tan Chen talk about an invisible group of nearly fifty-seven million Americans who get overlooked because they are "nearly poor." This group includes 21 percent of our nation's children.

When I reflect on what I heard in our hallway this evening, I recognize the enormous impact of being seen. We can't look the other way and imagine that the problems of the world don't exist and aren't ours to help solve. It seems to me that we may have to start looking at these invisible poor and those in need, especially the children, and like Jesus with Zacchaeus do something about it and invite them into our communities. Because, from what I am told, "It's great to be seen."

PRAYER

God of the visible and the invisible, make us stubborn and compassionate advocates of every one of your children.

Steve Camilleri, MAT
(Holy Ghost Catholic School, Hammond, LA)

The Authority of Jesus Questioned

Mark 11:27–33

Again Jesus and his disciples came to Jerusalem. As he was walking in the temple, the chief priests, the scribes, and the elders came to him and said, "By what authority are you doing these things? Who gave you this authority to do them?" Jesus said to them, "I will ask you one question. Answer me, and I will tell you by what authority I do these things. Did the baptism of John come from heaven, or was it of human origin? Answer me." They argued with one another, "If we say, 'From heaven,' he will say, 'Why then did you not believe him?' But shall we say, 'Of human origin?'"—they were afraid of the crowd, for all regarded John as truly a prophet. So they answered Jesus, "We do not know." And Jesus said to them, "Neither will I tell you by what authority I am doing these things."

Discipline. Exercise. Authority. I subscribe to the school of each. I take pride in the fact that I maintain a high standard of discipline in my classroom and in my personal life. I employ that sense of discipline to exercise the minds of my students and my physical self on a regular basis. I value and listen to authority; and as a teacher, I strive to use it wisely. These three fundamentals of my life recently came together in a powerful way when I read this gospel passage.

I approached the story using one of my least favorite disciplines: imaginative prayer, one of the hallmarks of Ignatian spirituality. Key insights about God came to Ignatius through his imagination. This method calls us to place ourselves fully within a story from the gospels. Admittedly, this practice has often been a struggle for me. Typically, I would complete it and feel disconnected, sometimes even empty. I never really met Jesus until I read this passage. Suddenly, there he was, a teacher like no other.

The story finds Jesus teaching in the temple. The chief priests and teachers of the Law of Moses are afraid of him because the crowds are completely amazed at his teaching. I place myself there. *Afraid of him? Of Jesus?* They question his authority and ask him what right he has to do and say such things. *What do they really fear? His influence? His authenticity? His ability to love?* I imagine myself as one of those astonished by this teacher. *What is he sharing with me? Is my heart burning?* I begin to long to be in the temple to sense the authority that Jesus brings to the world, to experience the powerful charisma, the enrapturing love, and the authority of this master teacher.

Through the discipline of this spiritual exercise of scriptural imagination, I met Christ the Teacher in a new way. May we daily meet and connect with him in our classrooms, at practice, and wherever our imaginations take us.

PRAYER

Lord Jesus, illuminate our minds and our hearts each and every day so we can "see you more clearly, follow you more nearly."

Anne Stricherz, MAT
(St. Ignatius College Prep, San Francisco, CA)

The Sheep and the Goats

Matthew 25:31–36, 40–41, 45

When the Son of Man comes in his glory, and all the angels with him, he will separate people one from another as a shepherd separates the sheep from the goats, and he will put the sheep at his right hand and the goats at the left. Then the king will say to those at his right hand, "Come, you that are blessed by my Father, inherit the kingdom; for I was hungry and you gave me food, I was thirsty and you gave me something to drink, I was a stranger and you welcomed me, I was naked and you gave me clothing, I was sick and you took care of me, I was in prison and you visited me. Just as you did it to one of the least of these who are members of my family, you did it to me." Then he will say to those at his left hand, "You that are accursed, depart from me into the eternal fire prepared for the devil and his angels; for just as you did not do it to one of the least of these, you did not do it to me."

This story raises the most disturbing of possibilities for us practicing Christians: we may have thought we were following Jesus' teaching our whole lives and yet have been totally wrong. It is as if we were expecting an "A" and found out on the final exam that we missed the most fundamental point of the class. What went wrong?

The "goats," it appears, are idolaters. They mistake the true God for a god of their own making. The goats cannot fathom Christ's presence in the needy in their midst. They close their hearts to the poor and in so doing fail to encounter the God revealed in Jesus—the God who can be loved only in serving the poor.

Christ the Teacher warns us about the danger of religious self-deception. We can go through the motions of Christianity without ever grasping its message. We can call ourselves Christians and, in ignoring the needy, turn away from the Christ we profess. The "sheep," on the other hand, by their compassionate response to the poor, welcome the Christ. Jesus cares not about our words but about our deeds, not about our piety but about our love.

PRAYER

God, in your mercy give us hearts that move us to actions of love.

Clark Power, EdD
(University of Notre Dame, Notre Dame, IN)

The Widow's Offering

Luke 21:1–4

Jesus looked up and saw rich people putting their gifts into the treasury; he also saw a poor widow put in two small copper coins. He said, "Truly I tell you, this poor widow has put in more than all of them; for all of them have contributed out of their abundance, but she out of her poverty has put in all she had to live on."

It was a Tuesday and I was exhausted. Labor Day weekend was a distant memory, and Thanksgiving still seemed far away. With practices, lesson plans, grading, and the typical classroom management woes churning through my mind, I walked into school that morning feeling more than defeated.

As I moved through the day with each of my religion classes, nothing dramatically improved. No shining light broke through the ceiling, doves certainly did not descend, and no students stood on their desks crying, "Oh Captain, my Captain!" But, as the last bell rang I realized that I had made it through. Even if my students would never know the struggle that it was for me to get out of bed that morning and drive to school, they had seen me there, present and teaching the Gospel as authentically as possible. I may not have been the most charismatic, funny, or engaging teacher that day, but simply in showing up and being present, I had given my students all that I could, and together we kept moving.

When I hear the gospel passage of the poor woman putting in her two coins, I think of this day and others like it when I feel that I have nothing of real significance to offer. I relate to her struggle and to her giving all that she had even when it paled in comparison to the gifts of those around her. I find comfort and encouragement in Jesus' words of praise, "She out of her poverty has put in all she had to live on." I find hope in the mere fact that Jesus was gazing lovingly upon her and noticed that she gave all she could.

We are not ever alone, and our offerings, no matter how small or meager, do not go unnoticed. And so, when we experience these "poor widow" days, we can be inspired both by her example and by that of Christ the Teacher. She encourages us to give out of our poverty, even as Christ affirms and challenges us to notice and acknowledge those who give out of their poverty. Whether we respond to the uneasy smile of someone struggling with issues at home or the distracted questions of a student having trouble listening, we are called to personally and publicly acknowledge the beauty of the gifts they have shared.

In Christ, the perfect teacher, we give all that we are able, and we accept and acknowledge the good that others share with us.

PRAYER

Loving God, thank you for your presence in and with us each day. As we continually pray for our daily bread, help us to return our offerings to you with faith and with gladness.

Margaret Morgan, MEd, MDiv
(Charlotte Catholic High School, Charlotte, NC)

Jesus Predicts His Death

John 12:23–26

Jesus said to his disciples, "The hour has come for the Son of Man to be glorified. Very truly, I tell you, unless a grain of wheat falls into the earth and dies, it remains just a single grain; but if it dies, it bears much fruit. Those who love their life lose it, and those who hate their life in this world will keep it for eternal life. Whoever serves me must follow me, and where I am, there will my servant be also. Whoever serves me, the Father will honor."

"Unless a grain of wheat falls into the earth and dies . . ." Often I focus on the verb *dies* so completely that I miss the all-important verb in front of it, *falls*. Perhaps the seed falling is as significant as the seed dying. A seed among many, sitting in the bag or the grain bin, can do nothing. It is the fall to the ground that continues the promise of new life.

Falling implies all those things that a leader of a classroom naturally dreads—a loss of control, an experience of letting go, a free-fall surrender. I often move in the opposite direction, seeking security and safety. I don't trust God to look out for the best interests of my students and me, so I have to take charge and make things happen. Jesus' strength was his openness to the Father's will. He loved the Father so much that whatever was needed, whatever was called for, he took on the challenge. Jesus followed the Father's agenda, regardless of whether the crowd would applaud or condemn. His obedience was a perfect gift of love.

I want to reach the point where nothing else matters but to do the will of the God I love. To trust that God will not lead me astray, will not leave me floundering. I want to give God the best I have to offer, no longer caring about looking foolish or worrying about the outcomes. Once I move as God directs me, the results will be miraculous.

To fall is the first step. May we surrender with joyful abandonment, giving of ourselves completely without holding back. Only then will the seed burst open and unbelievable abundance spring forth.

PRAYER

Lord, give us the courage to surrender our will completely, trusting in your promise of abundant living and everlasting life.

Donna Frazier, MEd, MA
(St. Francis Xavier School, Taos, MO)

Jesus Comforts His Disciples

John 14:1–4

Jesus said to his disciples, "Do not let your hearts be troubled. Trust in God, trust also in me. In my Father's house there are many dwelling-places. If it were not so, would I have told you that I go to prepare a place for you? And if I go and prepare a place for you, I will come again and will take you to myself, so that where I am, there you may be also."

For Christians, building trust in Christ doesn't work quite the same way as building trust in people. In human relationships, trust is conditional. It systematically builds as the evidence—and thereby our sense of assurance—builds. Our students' trust in us grows as they settle into our dependable daily routine, our reliable grading system, our consistent compassion toward them. But with Christ, trust is mostly unconditional, based more on faith than evidence. In this reading from Holy Week, Jesus has just given the disciples the disturbing news that he is going away. But he urges them not to be troubled but simply to trust him.

From the disciples' perspective, this must have been a tall order, straining the capacity of their faith.

On what previous experience could the disciples have built trust in these words that, although he was going away, they could count on his presence? Jesus was so unpredictable, so atypical. He turned the law on its ear, told stories that didn't make sense, had all the power of heaven at his fingertips—yet did nothing to overthrow Rome.

From our perspective, trusting God can be a tall order too. There's so much darkness in the world, so much evidence that seems to belie the existence of a good God. How can we truly trust him? The short answer is: *it's hard because we're human, but it's possible because of Christ.*

John's gospel assures us that trusting Christ the Teacher is possible because time after time he shows up. Not only does he seek to soothe his anxious students with powerful words of comfort and hope the night before he dies. Not only does he prove himself trustworthy by making good on his promise to die and rise again. But afterward, Jesus tracks down his fear-ridden friends as they huddle behind locked doors, finally enabling them to follow him with reckless, faith-filled abandon.

So it is with us. Christ the Teacher longs to address our gravest doubts, allay our wildest fears, and even come to us when we are too afraid to come to him. Trusting Christ isn't always easy, but by the strength of his presence, we *can* trust him. By faith, we can follow him wherever he leads.

PRAYER

Father in heaven, thank you for the gift of Jesus, the author of our faith and foundation of our trust. In his name build our trust in you today.

Ann Primus Berends
(University of Notre Dame, Notre Dame, IN)

ABIDING IN CHRIST

JOHN 15:1–5

Jesus said, "I am the true vine, and my Father is the vine-grower. He removes every branch in me that bears no fruit. Every branch that bears fruit he prunes to make it bear more fruit. You have already been cleansed by the word that I have spoken to you. Abide in me as I abide in you. Just as the branch cannot bear fruit by itself unless it abides in the vine, neither can you unless you abide in me. I am the vine, you are the branches. Those who abide in me and I in them bear much fruit, because apart from me you can do nothing."

Talk about the unexpected. God sent me to a tiny town in a state where I never thought I would live to teach subjects that were not my major in a struggling school that would close at the end of my first year. What in the world was God thinking? The year was far from perfect; I spent most of it *trying* to be a teacher, rather than actually *being* one. Somehow, though, my imperfections didn't matter. God allowed me to be a blessing—and to be blessed—anyway.

Not long after starting to teach, I saw God had a plan for me in the life of one of my students. He was small, and most of his peers called him scrawny or worse. He came to me for tutoring in math, but we both soon figured out that it wasn't math that brought him to me. He needed a listening ear. He was a "songwriter" for a "band," he told me. But over time, I learned that there was no band. And the songs were essentially suicide notes filled with sad, depressive thoughts. He gave me permission (although in this case, I didn't need it) to tell his mom that he was hurting, and his mom got him to counseling.

The school year ended, and I returned to graduate school, exhausted and uncertain, for my second summer of teacher training. Now I was the one who was sad and depressed. But some of the program staff rescued me, encouraging me to seek the help I needed. Not only had God used me during the school year as a blessing in the life of my student, but God blessed me during the summer through the helpful support of the people with whom I worked.

And that's not the end of the story. The biggest gift of all arrived when I returned to that tiny town. The "songwriter" wrote me a song with one line that I will never forget: "I am on this Earth because of you." God used me, a very imperfect teacher, to save the life of this songwriter. He is grown now, and we have lost touch, but he remains a reminder to me that God uses us whether we are ready or not. "Those who abide in me and I in them bear much fruit."

PRAYER

Dear Lord, please bring us ever closer to your eternal Love.

Michael Brennan, MEd
(St. Norbert Abbey, De Pere, WI)

The Last Supper

John 15:13–17

At the Last Supper, Jesus said to his disciples, "This is my commandment: love one another as I love you. No one has greater love than this, to lay down one's life for one's friends. You are my friends if you do what I command you. I have called you friends, because I have told you everything I have heard from my Father. It was not you who chose me, but I who chose you. This I command you: love one another."

When I look back on nearly three decades as a teacher, the most powerful sensation that strikes me is one of overwhelming gratitude. Above all, I feel gratitude for the unsurpassed gift of being invited into the richly textured lives of my students and, little by little, growing in friendship with them. Teaching is, ultimately, a sacrament of friendship—not in a superficial sense, but in the deepest sense of the word, the way Jesus used the word at the Last Supper: "I have called you friends."

I recall my first homeroom class, "*Tercero* C," at Saint George's College in Santiago, Chile. I was the newly ordained "gringo," patrolling the rows of a classroom of forty-three unruly boys and girls who spoke a language and shared a culture not my own. It was a classroom filled with life and laughter, always edging toward (or completely submerged in) utter pandemonium. I lost my temper regularly with these borderline hoodlums! But I loved them. I loved the "problem kids" especially—and they knew that.

During those days, I often ordered frequent offenders to my office for a private meeting, usually to read them the riot act. One time, I called a meeting with a normally quiet and docile student who had suddenly begun to act out. I was beside myself with confusion. When he arrived at the office, I asked what was going on with this uncharacteristic misbehavior. He reported that I always seemed so busy that he never really got a chance to talk with me. So he decided to misbehave. The only way to really spend time with me was in detention in my office!

This student was teaching me about what is really important. It's about relationship. Ultimately, it's about friendship. Teaching is a sacrament of friendship.

As I look back on my life as a teacher, I understand intensely what Jesus was experiencing even more completely. At the end of the day, the relationship of a teacher to his students is one of deep friendship. Perhaps that is why at the first Eucharist, this sacrament of thanksgiving, Jesus places at the center of his instruction his gratitude for the experience of friendship with his disciples. My most treasured gift as a teacher, and the most enduring, is the lifelong and life-transforming friendships I have received as a result of having been called to share in Christ's teaching ministry.

PRAYER

Christ, our ever-living Savior, what a gift it is that you call us your friends! Let our teaching ministry today be a sacrament of friendship that leads each student into a life-transforming relationship with you.

Fr. Tim Scully, C.S.C.
(Collegio St. George's, Santiago, Chile)

GETHSEMANE

MATTHEW 26:36–39

Then Jesus went with his disciples to a place called Gethsemane; and he said to them, "Sit here while I go over there and pray." He took with him Peter and the two sons of Zebedee, and began to be grieved and agitated. Then he said to them, "I am deeply grieved, even to death; remain here, and stay awake with me." And going a little farther, he threw himself on the ground and prayed, "My Father, if it is possible, let this cup pass from me; yet not what I want but what you want."

Jesus remains faithful to his ministry of teaching always, even through his passion and death. In his agony, he teaches us how to pray: to bring our pain, sorrow, and even our desire for control to God, but ultimately keep the Father's will at the center of our hearts. "I am deeply grieved . . . let this cup pass from me; yet, not what I want but what you want." Through this lesson on prayer, Jesus also shows us a transformative disposition toward life—that although we may not understand the meaning of our pain and suffering, God is somehow at work in it, and we must take up our cross and follow.

Such a disposition demands that, in our ministry of teaching, we help others see God at work in hardship. In the words of spiritual writer Henri Nouwen, "Ministry is the spiritual act of seeing and helping others see the face of a loving God even where nothing but darkness seems to be present." Put another way, students will watch how we respond to adversity in our own lives, how we carry our crosses. Do we do so with humble, trusting hearts?

As teachers, we can play a critical role in helping our students cope with hardship in a way that ultimately draws them closer to God. When we, like Christ in Gethsemane, approach our lives with a spirit of thanksgiving for God's will at work in our suffering, we powerfully model this disposition for our students. And in the process, our own importance is diminished; our witness communicates the presence of God, even in the midst of hardship, and the importance of living a Christ-centered life.

PRAYER

Lord, help me to keep your will at the center of my heart even amid pain and suffering, just as Jesus did at Gethsemane.

Sarah Lamphier, MEd
(St. Anthony Catholic School, Harlingen, TX)

Climbing toward Golgotha

Luke 23:24–27

Pilate gave his verdict that the crowd's demand for Jesus' death should be granted. He released the man they asked for, the one who had been put in prison for insurrection and murder, and he handed Jesus over as they wished. As they led him away, they seized a man, Simon of Cyrene, who was coming from the country, and they laid the cross on him, and made him carry it behind Jesus. A great number of the people followed him, and among them were women who were beating their breasts and wailing for him.

I try to imagine myself in Simon's shoes. I am visiting the big city on some business, probably a bit miffed that the street is clogged with people who are getting in the way of my plans. Abruptly and without volunteering, I am pressed into strenuous labor, carrying a cross for a man about whom I know nothing to the place where he will be crucified. I can only imagine the experience of many emotions, ranging from annoyance to pity to sadness.

We have all, assuredly, been asked to carry others' crosses from time to time. This is part of the Christian life. *Take up your cross and follow me.* Usually, however, we have a chance to decide whether or not to take on someone else's burden. We have the opportunity to say yes or no. In Simon's case, he is simply plucked out of the crowd and pressed into immediate service, without any sort of assent.

As a teacher, I knew that my job was one of service; I knew that I would work tirelessly to give my students the chance to succeed academically as well as provide them the emotional and spiritual support they deserved. When I said yes to being a teacher, it was a conscious decision to say yes to helping my middle school students carry whatever crosses that burdened them. I knew that it would be difficult, and sometimes it was. Sometimes the responsibility became a cross of its own.

But what struck me time and time again was the sudden, unexpected occasion, much like the one experienced by Simon from Cyrene, when the cross a student carried was abruptly forced upon me, and I was invited—but really, pressed—to carry it for awhile. This was a moment of grace that mysteriously, as with Simon, brought me face-to-face with Jesus.

When I think about Christ the Teacher, I reflect upon how Christ taught me about the heart of a true servant, helping me carry the cross of another, even if I was unprepared or my own cross felt too heavy to bear.

PRAYER

Jesus, help me to serve, carrying my brothers' and sisters' crosses, in and with love.

Aaron Wall, MEd
(San Xavier Mission School, Tucson, AZ)

Jesus' Crucifixion

Luke 23:33–37

When they came to the place called Skull, they crucified Jesus there, and the criminals, one on the right side, the other on the left. Jesus said, "Father forgive them, for they don't know what they are doing." They cast lots in order to divide up his garments. The people stood watching. But the leaders kept mocking. They said, "He saved others. Let him save himself if this is God's Messiah, the elect one!" The soldiers also approached and mocked him. They offered him vinegar and said, "If you are the king of the Jews, save yourself!"

Before I became a teacher, I never considered that it would sometimes be a lonely profession in which I would often have to forgive my students for their behavior. I envisioned my classroom productively bustling with young people passionate about their learning. I pictured the faculty lounge alive with voices of educators exchanging instructional techniques over the low hum of the photocopier. Teaching is so often such a communal profession. Therefore, it came as a total shock one autumn Friday afternoon, while I stood in front of a full classroom, that I suddenly felt completely alone and increasingly frustrated with my students.

I taught during the last period of the day, a football game was looming on the horizon that evening, and my eleventh-grade morality class was the only obstacle between my students and their weekend freedom. They showed no desire to sit quietly and follow my instructions or participate in my lesson activities. As I wrote the class agenda on the board, I became acutely aware of my own isolation and dwindling patience amid a room of twenty-five rambunctious teenagers. I could only turn to God and offer the next fifty minutes of my day—and my students—to his care.

As I read today's passage on the crucifixion, my heart understands that Christ experienced true loneliness and isolation on the cross. He was mocked and criticized as he suffered the cost of our human sinfulness. Nonetheless, he forgave the behavior of his persecutors, saying, "They don't know what they are doing." Christ gave his life over for them.

I have learned that encountering obstinate, distracted, and at times disrespectful behavior from students is as much a part of teaching as the triumphs and successes. If Christ found the strength in his loneliest hour to forgive and give up his life for the people responsible for putting him to death, should I not also find the strength to forgive and give my day's work over for my students' sometimes misguided behavior?

PRAYER

Thank you, Lord Jesus, that with you I am never alone. As you gave and forgave in your loneliest hour, help me do the same today.

Michael Suso, MEd
(Pensacola Catholic High School, Pensacola, FL)

Jesus Appears to the Women

Matthew 28:1–10

After the Sabbath, as the first day of the week was dawning, Mary Magdalene and the other Mary went to see the tomb. And suddenly there was a great earthquake; for an angel of the Lord, descending from heaven, came and rolled back the stone and sat on it. The angel said to the women, "Do not be afraid; I know that you are looking for Jesus who was crucified. He is not here; for he has been raised, as he said. Come, see the place where he lay. Then go quickly and tell his disciples, 'He has been raised from the dead, and indeed he is going ahead of you to Galilee; there you will see him.' This is my message for you." So the women left the tomb quickly with fear and great joy, and ran to tell his disciples. Suddenly Jesus met them and said, "Greetings!" And they came to him, took hold of his feet, and worshipped him. Then Jesus said to them, "Do not be afraid; go and tell my brothers to go to Galilee; there they will see me."

I've heard somewhere that joy is God's life echoing within us. I imagine that this was never truer than when Mary Magdalene and the other Mary were sprinting away from the empty tomb, bubbling over with the news of Christ's resurrection. With the angel's voice still ringing in their ears—and through their souls—I can only imagine their adrenaline rushing and their hearts pounding with very human manifestations of joy. The conviction that God's life is more powerful than death was echoing within them.

But Matthew tells us that joy wasn't the only emotion coursing through their veins that morning. They also experienced the fear that inevitably comes with the unknown. They ran "with fear and great joy." What could this mean? What power is at work?

When Jesus meets the women on their way, his first words order their fear away: "Do not be afraid." Yet, Jesus' next admonition may be most important for understanding the women's joy. To paraphrase, Jesus simply says, "Go spread the news of the Resurrection, and invite my friends to an encounter with the Risen Lord."

This second directive once again awakens the echo of God's life within the women. Christ's invitation to action, evangelization, and ministry—ultimately, an invitation to joy—removes the paralysis of fear. This invitation spreads joy to the Church, for God's life indeed echoes among us today.

Christ the Teacher does not simply order our fear away. Rather, through his invitation to go and spread the Gospel message, Christ frees us from our fears and teaches us a true path to joy.

PRAYER

Father, show us the path to true joy as we bring others to you.

Chuck Lamphier, MEd, MNA
(Saint Joseph Academy, Brownsville, TX)

Jesus Appears to Mary Magdalene

John 20:13–19

The angels said to (Mary Magdalene) "Woman, why are you weeping?" She said to them, "They have taken away my Lord, and I do not know where they have laid him." When she had said this, she turned around and saw Jesus standing there, but she did not know that it was Jesus. Jesus said to her, "Woman, why are you weeping? Whom are you looking for?" Supposing him to be the gardener, she said to him, "Sir, if you have carried him away, tell me where you have laid him, and I will take him away." Jesus said to her, "Mary!" She turned and said to him in Hebrew, "Rabbouni!" (which means Teacher). Jesus said to her, "Do not hold on to me, because I have not yet ascended to the Father. But go to my disciples and say to them, 'I am ascending to my Father and your Father, to my God and your God.'" Mary Magdalene went and announced to the disciples, "I have seen the Lord"; and she told them that he had said these things to her.

Iris!" "Noah!" "Phong!" "Dionisio!" "Saraswati!" "LaToya!" Just think about it, every day across the globe millions of teachers call out billions of student names. Each of us can remember the distinct feeling of hearing our names called out by a teacher—snapping us out of ourselves and stretching us into a more attentive and alert state of mind.

"What's the answer?" "Pay attention!" "Are you ok?" Every second of every day, teachers are calling upon students by name, inviting them—sometimes pulling them, kicking and screaming!—into deeper relationships with the world, their neighbors, and themselves. Just imagine this constant chorus of names—Lamar, Benito, Jules—echoing from classrooms, tents, and places of learning throughout the world. Imagine the teachable moments streaming from each of these personal callings: "Jean-Pierre . . ." "Malik . . ." "Fadiya . . ."

"Mary!" With one word, Jesus invites Mary Magdalene into a place of greater understanding. At the beginning of this scene, Mary is driven by one concern: to find the missing body of Jesus. Barreling down the tracks of this singular quest, Mary fails to recognize the incredible moment of learning before her very eyes. Then she hears her name and awakens, becoming present to her "Rabboni," Christ the Teacher.

At this point the true lesson begins. "Do not hold on to me," Jesus cautions, revealing that through the

Passion and the Cross, he is no longer just a wise and thoughtful Rabboni; he is the risen Lord! Then he adds, "Go instead to my disciples and say to them . . ." Here Jesus calls Mary into a deeper relationship with him as her Savior and bids her to spread the word.

As with Mary, we are called to be present to Christ the Teacher and to share the revolutionary news that Jesus is Lord. As Christian teachers, we must call our students by name—Alejandro, Raekwon, Mary—into such moments of personal conversion every day.

PRAYER

Christ our Savior, help us to be attentive to your presence and active in sharing your gospel message today.

Tony DeSapio, MEd
(St. Paul School, Memphis, TN)

Jesus on the Road to Emmaus

Luke 24:13–18, 30–31

Now on that same day two of Jesus' followers were going to a village called Emmaus and talking with each other about all these things that had happened when Jesus died. While they were talking, Jesus himself came and went with them, but their eyes were kept from recognizing him. And he said to them, "What are you discussing?" They stood still, looking sad, and one of them answered, "Are you the only stranger in Jerusalem who does not know the things that have taken place there in these days?" Later, when he was at the table with them, he took bread, blessed and broke it, and gave it to them. Then their eyes were opened, and they recognized him.

As principals and teachers we must always remember that we are not alone. At times the road may appear long and lonely, but God will always be at our side in the form of our students, the teacher across the hall, our family, and every time we celebrate Communion in the breaking of the bread.

As I think about the journey of the Christian teacher, I identify with the disciples in this famous passage. When we are juggling all that we have to do, it is easy to lose sight of an opportunity to experience Christ, who is often walking right beside us. And so we challenge ourselves to start each day with some quiet time to open our hearts to seeing each relationship and each event as a chance to encounter Christ. Whatever the situation, we ask ourselves: How can we find Christ here, in this person, in this moment? Can we find him during a difficult parent meeting, a discipline meeting with a student, dealing with finances, a teacher who needs help seeing the mission, or balancing family time and school? Do we find him in a student receiving honor roll for the first time, a student winning a game, having someone hold the door for us, receiving a simple smile, or going to Mass? And how can we allow other persons to see Christ in us, even when what we have to say may not be what they want to hear?

Like the disciples on the road to Emmaus, we as teachers have roads to travel. The goal is to walk together, sharing in each other's struggles, nourishing each other's souls, discovering the sometimes invisible presence of Christ in our midst. This way, like these two disciples who run back to Jerusalem to tell of the miracle that has occurred, we can go even further than we thought possible.

Let's take time to be still today, asking that our hearts and eyes be open to the presence of Christ along the road before us and to receiving Christ's call to serve and to teach.

PRAYER

Christ our Teacher, continue to ignite our passion for Christian education, making us ever aware that you are with us every step of the way.

Patrick O'Sullivan, MAT, MA
(Bishop Dunne Catholic School, Dallas, TX)

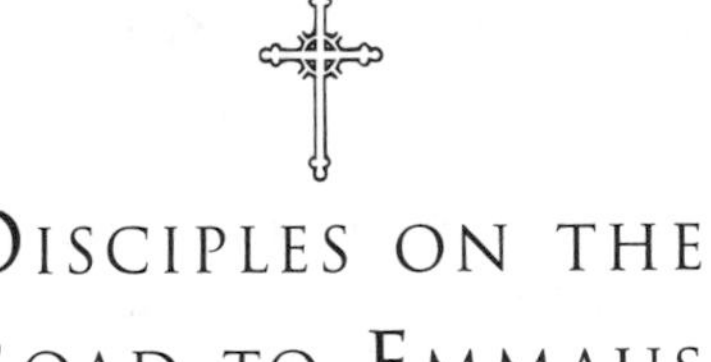

Disciples on the Road to Emmaus

Luke 24:30–35

When Jesus was at the table with the two disciples, he took bread, blessed and broke it, and gave it to them. Then their eyes were opened, and they recognized him; and he vanished from their sight. They said to each other, "Were not our hearts burning within us while he was talking to us on the road, while he was opening the scriptures to us?" That same hour they got up and returned to Jerusalem; and they found the Eleven and their companions gathered together. They were saying, "The Lord has risen indeed, and he has appeared to Simon!" Then they told what had happened on the road, and how he had been made known to them in the breaking of the bread.

Were not our hearts burning within us?" ask the two disciples after recognizing Jesus on the road to Emmaus. Christ helps the disciples recognize and understand this burning of their hearts at the conclusion of their shared journey. When he first joins them on the road, Jesus asks them about the topic of their conversation. Horrified at his apparent ignorance of the latest news, they recount the events of Good Friday and Easter morning but do not know how to interpret the empty tomb. Jesus interprets the scriptures for them, explaining the words of the prophets and the glory of the Resurrection. The disciples press him to stay the evening with them and finally recognize Christ when he celebrates the Eucharist at table.

At the point of recognition the disciples realize their hearts were burning for him all along. Interestingly, they had knowledge of the facts—the crucifixion, the burial, and the empty tomb—yet they did not know the truth. Even though their hearts were on fire, yearning for the truth, they could not access it until Jesus revealed himself to them through scripture and sacrament.

Regardless of our content area, we teach children facts. Yet, Christ the Teacher on the road to Emmaus reminds us that we also teach children truth and help them understand what is divinely revealed through fact. As Christian educators, we bear the responsibility to help our students recognize the burning of their own hearts for truth, teaching as Jesus did that we can come to know God more fully through the sacred Word and traditions of the Church.

Every child merits a quality education. Our children also deserve a quality Christian education. What our students do with that education is their decision, but we can hope and pray that they, like the two disciples, will return to their friends and tell "what had happened on the road, and how he had been made known to them in the breaking of the bread."

PRAYER

Jesus, keep our hearts burning within us,
this day and always.

Virginia Dybicz, MEd
(St. Patrick Catholic High School, Biloxi, MS)

Teaching Resurrection

Luke 24:36–37, 39, 41–46, 48–49

While the disciples were talking about Jesus' death and resurrection, Jesus himself stood among them and said to them, "Peace be with you." They were startled and terrified, and thought that they were seeing a ghost. He said to them, "Look at my hands and my feet; see that it is I myself. Touch me and see; for a ghost does not have flesh and bones as you see that I have." While in their joy they were disbelieving and still wondering, he said to them, "Have you anything here to eat?" They gave him a piece of broiled fish, and he took it and ate in their presence. Then he said to them, "These are my words that I spoke to you while I was still with you—that everything written about me in the law of Moses, the prophets, and the psalms must be fulfilled." Then he opened their minds to understand the Scriptures, and he said to them, "You are witnesses of these things. And see, I am sending upon you what my Father promised; so stay here in the city until you have been clothed with power from on high."

The Christian classroom is a school of Resurrection. To some this might seem a narrow charge, but to the Christian educator, Christ risen from the dead is the source of the curriculum and the sum of the learning.

Christ vanquished death not only to witness to life but to become life's very teacher, revealing a depth to life heretofore unknown. The disciples, his earnest students, were broken in their knowledge. Part of them had died on Calvary too. What they had known was no longer. For certain, Christ's reappearance was troubling. Yet, Christ the Teacher meets them in their questioning. He knows their fears, their faults, and their devastation at his death. And so Christ's presentation of the nail marks in his hands and feet and his eating a piece of fish are not merely evidential proofs of his resurrection, but the first lesson of a pedagogy of new life. Christ draws out wholeness from the broken knowledge in his students; he teaches them that learning requires dying and rising again.

Christian schools teach the Resurrection because never does an error, mistake, confusion, or conceptual challenge necessarily go unredeemed. These might be crosses and require a certain dying, but only so that students and teachers might be raised alike to new and lifelong knowledge. Resurrection for us is the pedagogy, a daily practice that draws every subject and learning through death to new life. For when we have practiced it enough from day to day, we shall discover that all the way along our Lord has been teaching us the lesson of that final resurrection when we too will rise to die no more.

PRAYER

Teach us, Lord, the lessons of resurrection today.

Fr. Kevin Grove, C.S.C.
(Christ the King Catholic Parish and School, South Bend, IN)

Doubting Thomas

John 20:24–29

But Thomas (who was called the Twin), one of the Twelve, was not with the disciples when Jesus appeared to them in the house. So the others told Thomas, "We have seen the Lord." But he said to them, "Unless I see the mark of the nails in his hands, and put my finger in the mark of the nails and my hand in his side, I will not believe." A week later his disciples were again in the house, and Thomas was with them. Although the doors were shut, Jesus came and stood among them and said, "Peace be with you." Then he said to Thomas, "Put your finger here and see my hands. Reach out your hand and put it in my side. Do not doubt but believe." Thomas answered him, "My Lord and my God!" Jesus said to him, "Have you believed because you have seen me? Blessed are those who have not seen and yet have come to believe."

The original prophecy was: "They shall name him Emmanuel, which means 'God is with us.'" Jesus' entire life was the fulfillment of this urgent message—God now lives among us. Even in this resurrection account, we are reminded of how Christ the Teacher confirms this new reality. Jesus again appears to the disciples—who out of fear, despite having already received the gift of the Holy Spirit, remained locked away in the upper room. Jesus teaches by example, by encounter, by revealing that nothing, not even death, can prevent him from being with them. With the simple word "peace" and the sharing of his wounds, Jesus does not scold Thomas or the others for not understanding his lessons about who he is or what he needed to do. Rather, he simply comes to them again, inviting them into deeper communion with him.

Ultimately, in sharing the wounds and being present even in the darkest, most fearful places, Christ the Teacher models the gift of belief, which is knowing that God is with us even though we may not feel it or understand how.

So, thank God for Thomas, who was absent for the first resurrection encounter. His desire to touch and see Jesus actually gave Jesus the excuse to come back and not only teach him but reengage the others whose knowledge and belief were incomplete. It is Christ's persistence, patience, and ability to encounter his students where they are that ultimately freed them to be themselves, to accept Christ's invitation, and finally to leave the upper room and share this gift of faith, however fragile, with others. May we too be freed, by Christ's persistent and invincible teaching, to be who we are and to see our students as they really are, and in doing so share this most incredible gift: *God is with us.*

PRAYER

Christ, help us to touch and see you today. Let our hearts be filled with the gratitude in knowing that you find us, hear us, and bring us healing.

Fr. Sean McGraw, C.S.C.
(University of Notre Dame, Notre Dame, IN)

I Am with You Always

Matthew 28:18–20

And Jesus came and said to them, "All authority in heaven and on earth has been given to me. Go therefore and make disciples of all nations, baptizing them in the name of the Father and of the Son and of the Holy Spirit, and teaching them to obey everything that I have commanded you. And remember, I am with you always, to the end of the age."

I'm uncertain sometimes where the lines between my students and me ought to be drawn—teaching is a profession, but it is also a ministry, and finding the balance is tricky. My first teaching job was with the Daughters of Mary, Help of Christians, Salesians whose charism centers on accompaniment. They do their jobs by being fully present to their students and community. Each student's glories and heartbreaks are the sisters' as well. When there is success or triumph in the community, the sisters celebrate with the families. When there is challenge or tragedy, they stand or kneel alongside the people they serve. They are simply present. The statement is clear: teaching is not just a job, and students are not just bodies in a desk. They are human souls, and they themselves—not simply their learning—are worth my time and attention.

Jesus sends us the same message in his last words to his disciples before departing from them. His primary activity while on earth, up until the very end, was teaching, and he did so with unprecedented and enduring effects. But he doesn't stop at instruction; he continues to teach us after his ascension by accompanying us. Christ treks our mountains and valleys, attends to each of our highs and lows, and is present to us even as he continues to work in us, teach us, teach others through us, and build up his kingdom. We accept his lessons because he has accepted us. We follow him because he has taken up our journey. He accompanies us always "to the end of the age."

PRAYER

Jesus, guide us and teach us so we can see you present in our lives and be your presence for others.

Andrea Cisneros, MEd
(Guadalupe Regional Middle School, Brownsville, TX)

The Commissioning of the Disciples

Matthew 28:16–20

Meanwhile the eleven disciples set out for Galilee, to the mountain where Jesus had arranged to meet them. When they saw him they fell down before him, though some hesitated. Jesus came up and spoke to them. He said, "All authority in heaven and on earth has been given to me. Go, therefore, make disciples of all the nations; baptize them in the name of the Father and of the Son and of the Holy Spirit, and teach them to observe all the commands I gave you. And know that I am with you always; yes, to the end of time."

When he was eighty-seven years old, still working vigorously—though already among the most famous and accomplished artists in history—Michelangelo wrote a note to himself in his journal: *Ancora imparo*, or, "Still, I learn."

In this note we get a glimpse of how the creator of the *Pietà*, David, and the Sistine Chapel experienced Christ's assurance that he is with us always and in all things. Michelangelo recognized that God, who created all things and became incarnate in Jesus, is truly present in all things. This awareness, this act of faith, instilled in him a thirst for knowledge and infused his work with the glory of God.

Ancora imparo describes too the mind-set of the ideal teacher who believes what Jesus told his disciples: "I am with you always." As witnesses to Christ's constant presence in the world, we (and our students) are never finished learning. Since God is in all things, the more we come to know about the world and its people, the more we come to know God, and the more our own work becomes infused with the glory of God. Teaching and learning are, indeed, sacred endeavors.

Here the unique capacity of Christian schoolteachers to carry out Christ's great commission—"Go, therefore, and teach"—becomes clear. Our lessons—whether in grammar, chemistry, or religion class—are sacred. As our students come to know the world and its people—through their study of science, math, literature, history, and the faith—they come to know God. For Christian schoolteachers, *ancora imparo* means that education is a process of sanctification. And it's a process that never ends. God willing, we'll be learning until we're eighty-seven and well beyond—"to the end of time!"

PRAYER

Lord, give us eyes of faith, that by learning more about the world and the people in it, we might come to see God in all things.

Christian Dallavis, PhD
(Mercy Cross Catholic School, Biloxi, MS)

The Great Commission

Matthew 28:18–20

And Jesus came and said to them, "All authority in heaven and on earth has been given to me. Go therefore and make disciples of all nations, baptizing them in the name of the Father and of the Son and of the Holy Spirit, and teaching them to obey everything that I have commanded you. And remember, I am with you always, to the end of the age."

A skilled teacher knows how to get the ball rolling. More importantly, she also knows how to ensure that, by the end of the course, she will be only one among many who knows how to roll the ball. She gives her students the information, support, and freedom they need to be successful not only in her classroom but also in her absence, whether at home doing their homework or moving forward into the next year of school.

Jesus too, as revealed in this passage, knows the value of the teaching strategy "model, coach, fade." He spends three years demonstrating to his apostles the goals he wants to achieve in the world; he assigns to them the ever-increasing responsibility of preaching, healing, and granting forgiveness; he gives them the parting gift of language and offers them the opportunity to keep in touch via the Eucharist. Then, even though the apostles are nervous, he hands them the reins.

Like rookie teachers, the apostles are sent into the world with little more than the sandals on their feet and the hope in their hearts. Although they have witnessed the peerless pedagogy of Christ the Teacher, they simply do not have the teaching experience that Jesus does. But they, being many, do have something that Jesus values so much that he is even willing to depart and leave the Church, the earthly presence of God, in their hands: the ability to be present—physically, sacramentally present—in all places at a single time. In this way, the apostles, and their companions and successors, can make "disciples of all nations"—and this all-encompassing command alone captures the breadth of Jesus' love. We, as Christian schoolteachers, administrators, and supporters, are called to do our part in our corner of the world. Go, therefore, and teach.

PRAYER

Lord, help us to instill a sense of mission in our students so that they may continue to spread the Gospel message, even to the ends of the earth.

Kate Nienaber, MEd
(Father Ryan High School, Nashville, TN)

REFERENCES

"Jesus Heals the Woman Crippled by a Spirit" (p. 99)
Johnson, Elizabeth A. *Consider Jesus* (New York: Crossroad Publishing Company, 1990), 108.

"The Mother of James and John" (p. 132)
Bonhoeffer, Dietrich. *Life Together* (New York: Harper and Row, Inc., 1954), 91.

"Zacchaeus the Tax Collector" (p. 143)
Newman, Catherine S., and Victor Tan Chen. *The Missing Class* (Boston: Beacon Press, 2007), 3.

"Gethsemane" (p. 165)
Nouwen, Henri J. M. "The Monk and the Cripple," *America: The National Catholic Weekly*, March 15, 1980, http://www.americamagazine.org/content/article.cfm?article_id=12184.

ABOUT THE ALLIANCE FOR CATHOLIC EDUCATION

The Alliance for Catholic Education (ACE), housed in the Institute for Educational Initiatives at the University of Notre Dame, exists for one purpose: to strengthen and sustain Catholic schools. This closely-knit, multigenerational program—honored by the White House, emulated by other universities, and growing in its impact and spectrum of services—engages people who are passionate about meeting the needs of under-resourced elementary and secondary schools around the globe. Over the years, the program has become one of Notre Dame's best known "exports." It can be found in hundreds of US schools, dozens of Catholic dioceses, and several foreign countries.

ACE began in 1993 as a two-year service program (now called ACE Service through Teaching) that offered committed and successful college graduates the opportunity to serve as full-time teachers in under-resourced Catholic schools. Because good teachers need excellent formation, ACE prepares its teachers in an innovative Master of Education program at Notre Dame, which brings them to campus for two summers of intensive training and then sends them out into classrooms during the school year. These teachers represent a broad variety of undergraduate disciplines, with a diverse set of backgrounds and experiences. While teaching, they live in small Christian communities of four to seven members and together share the many challenges and rewards of beginning teaching. Supported throughout the year by both pastoral and academic staff at Notre Dame, ACE teachers develop their professional skills and personal spirituality in the context of community, sharing with one another the journey of becoming committed Catholic school teachers.

ACE Service through Teaching has spawned numerous kindred programs by responding to emerging needs within and surrounding Catholic schools. These include formation for teachers and administrators, licensure in English as a Second Language and Teaching Exceptional Children, professional consulting services that are customized to help Catholic schools confront challenges such as participating in federal grant programs and strengthening curriculum and instruction, and outreach opportunities that galvanize all sorts of Catholic school supporters who want to collaborate in addressing key concerns. ACE is also addressing timely subjects for a growing grid of efforts, including parental choice advocacy, urgent educational trends (both local and global), and increasing access for Latino children and their families to US Catholic education.

The work of ACE to confront today's challenges in Catholic schools is enhancing lives all around. And as the nearly two thousand graduates and advocates like to say, "We're just getting started!"

REFLECTIONS AND CONTRIBUTORS INDEX

SUBJECT INDEX

The University of Notre Dame's Alliance for Catholic Education (ACE), sustains and strengthens under-resourced Catholic schools through leadership formation, research, and professional service to ensure that all children, especially those from low-income families, have the opportunity to experience the gift of an excellent Catholic education. The ACE website can be visited online at http//ace.nd.edu.

Rev. Louis A. DelFra, C.S.C., is a priest in the Congregation of Holy Cross and directs biblical studies for campus ministry at the University of Notre Dame. He also serves as director of pastoral life for the Alliance for Catholic Education. DelFra has also served as associate director for the ACE Program, associate pastor at Holy Redeemer Parish and School in Portland, Oregon, and as a middle school and high school teacher at a Catholic school in Philadelphia. He received his undergraduate and master's degrees from the University of Notre Dame.

Ann Primus Berends is associate director for ACE Advocates for Catholic Schools at the University of Notre Dame. She obtained her bachelor's degree in English from Calvin College and has worked for more than twenty-five years as a writer and editor in both the public and private sectors.

Founded in 1865, Ave Maria Press, a ministry of the Congregation of Holy Cross, is a Catholic publishing company that serves the spiritual and formative needs of the Church and its schools, institutions, and ministers; Christian individuals and families; and others seeking spiritual nourishment.

For a complete listing of titles from

Ave Maria Press

Sorin Books

Forest of Peace

Christian Classics

visit www.avemariapress.com

ave maria press® / Notre Dame, IN 46556
A Ministry of the United States Province of Holy Cross